Pioneer
Pentecostal Women
Volume III

by Mary Wallace

Pioneer Pentecostal Women
Volume III

by Mary Wallace

© 2003, Word Aflame Press
Hazelwood, MO 63042-2299

ISBN 1-56722-617-5

Cover Design by Paul Povolni

All Scripture quotations in this book are from the King James Version of the Bible unless otherwise identified.

Printed in United States of America

Printed by

WORD AFLAME®PRESS
8855 DUNN ROAD
HAZELWOOD, MO 63042-2299

Contents

Foreword

Alfred Tennyson wrote, "The world knows nothing of its greatest men," and but for Mary Wallace we would know nothing of some of the greatest women (and men) in our Pentecostal movement. She has contributed much to the history of our movement in researching the lives of many who lived in former years and have passed from active duty on life's scene. But for her diligence and desire to remember them, Christians of today would know nothing about them—only a choice few who remembered.

The women featured in this book served their generation well. They lived in challenging times, were confronted with decisions, and made commitments unknown to this generation. Some were mightily used of God in ministry; others were helpmeets to their husbands in ministry. Still others were godly homemakers who gave themselves to their families and were rewarded by seeing their children (even grandchildren) used of God in various positions and ministry.

My friendship with Mary Wallace began as our paths crossed at various General Conference functions while her husband was manager of the Pentecostal Publishing House. Our friendship deepened during the early days of getting our Ladies Ministries' magazine, *Reflections*, launched and published. Each time I would go to World Evangelism Center to work on the magazine and consult with the editor in chief, J. L. Hall, Mary and I would manage to have lunch together. She was working for Word Aflame. Her interest in the magazine and her recommendations and advice were very much appreciated by me, a novice editor.

She and her husband visited the church my husband pastored in Collinsville, Oklahoma, one weekend. She spoke for our mother/daughter banquet. It was a special treat to have them with us. While in the area, Mary visited the C. A. Nelsons in Claremore, Oklahoma, and gleaned material for the book *It's Real*.

She is the author of seventeen books. One of her latest books is a devotional entitled *Light for Living*. Each day's writing gives inspirational quotes from various sources, with comments and references to mutual friends and acquaintances. It seemed that as I read it I was having a short visit with her each morning.

"There is in every true woman's heart a spark of heavenly fire, which lies dormant in the broad daylight of prosperity, but which kindles up, and beams and blazes in the dark hour of adversity" (Washington Irving). May the biographies of these special ladies inspire each of you as you read of their courage, commitment, and challenges. These were women of "like passion" such as you and I. They just experienced life in a different era. We, too, can be women who are vessels of honor as they were.

Thank you, Mary, for another book of history, enlightenment, and inspiration.

Melissa A. Anderson, Secretary
Ladies Ministries of the
United Pentecostal Church International and
Editor of *Reflections*

CHAPTER One

Ila Ashcraft

"Who can find a virtuous woman? for her price is far above rubies" (Proverbs 31:10).

Ila Ashcraft, a large woman, dressed with simplicity in subdued colors suitable, she said, for a lady preacher. She favored hat and gloves. She had a translucent complexion, blue eyes, and black hair that prematurely turned to silver. She had two claims to beauty—her radiant smile and her graceful hands. She always carried a frilly handkerchief, usually one someone had crocheted for her. She used it to emphasize a point while preaching or to wipe her tears. It was almost a trademark.

Ila loved people, and God's children were her children. Young or old, it made no difference, but she had an affinity for small children and young people. They flocked around her and most of them called her Aunt Ila. One little girl told her mother, "If anything happens to you, I'm going to live with Aunt Ila."

A young mother said, "There was never anyone like Sister Ila for caring for people."

For example, six-year-old Melba had been bitten on the head by a spider. Her head swelled and she had been blind for three days. Ila insisted that the family stay in her home, and they prayed until midnight. After Ila had gone to bed, the mother sat by Melba's bed. Melba awoke around three o'clock and said she saw something white. This frightened her mother until she realized that Melba saw the moon shining through the window. The first thing Melba wanted to do was "tell Aunt Ila."

Because Sister Ila cared for young people, she often had the opportunity to counsel them. One teenager named Eileen was interested in a boy who came to church but was not a Christian. When he came to the altar, she put forth the argument, hoping for Aunt Ila's approval, that he had repented and thus was acceptable. Ila told her, "Yes, hon, but this brings to mind the story I've heard many times. There was a young man that was in the altar every night, and the minister came to him and said, 'It's so good that you are seeking salvation.'

"'Salvation?' the boy exclaimed. 'I'm seeking Sal Johnson!'"

On another occasion, a young mother was nervous, tense, and in need of rest. The tension was transmitted to her infant son, and he could nap for only short periods of time. Ila laid baby Larry on her lap, letting him grasp her thumbs in his little fists, as she sang, "I've got a mansion just over the hilltop." The baby was mesmerized and soon fell into a relaxed sleep that lasted over an hour.

Ila also ministered to children. Twelve-year-old Shirley thought God didn't love her and had forgotten all about her. Ila showed her Isaiah 49:16 and assured her that God loved her and couldn't possibly forget her because He had written her name in the palm of His hand.

Having no children of her own, Ila sometimes "adopted" a daughter. A despondent young wife, whose soldier husband was stationed overseas, lived in an apartment next door to the church parsonage. She had no family. Ila told her, "I'm a childless woman and you are a motherless child. Isn't God good to let us live so close to one another?"

The lonely girl smiled through her tears as she basked in the light of motherly love.

And so her life was lived.

*   *   *   *   *

Ila Thelma was born February 23, 1907, at Wetumka, Oklahoma, to Y. Z. and Viola Bates Vaughan. She was the second child in the family of eight children.

Y. Z. moved his family to the Morris area in 1917. They did not attend church regularly although Mr. Vaughan was a Methodist and Mrs. Vaughan had belonged to the Church of Christ.

During Ila's senior school year, she was invited to attend the Pentecostal church with a group of young people. She was converted and received the Holy Ghost and was later instrumental in her parents' conversion.

There was never a question in Ila's mind about the direction that her life would take. She knew from the time she received the Holy Ghost that she would be involved in God's work. It was just a matter of when and where. So when Willa Peters asked her and Gladys Smith to go to the Lake View community near St. Paul, Kansas, to work in a revival, she did not hesitate.

They prayed before embarking on their journey in December 1928, and God surely dispatched a guardian angel to protect them. The evangelistic trio, all girls in their twenties, traveled in a Model T with a balky battery on unpaved roads. When they stopped, they parked the car in a place so it could be pushed should it refuse to start, but the old car didn't miss a tap.

It rained, and as they neared Lake View, they came to a section of road that had great hunks dug out and piled to the side. There was no detour sign, so they started through. They crept through the mud at a snail's pace, skirting the deep holes in the road. As they approached an old bridge, Ila, whose keen wit kept them laughing, said, "There's the bridge that the ghost walks across at midnight. Let's hurry before he gets here!"

The people were astonished when they arrived safely. The road was impassable and closed to traffic. They never knew what happened to the sign.

Sister Bill, as Willa was called, had been advised to start the services at eight o'clock because "no one will come any earlier," but she announced services for seven-thirty anyway. At dusk the people could be seen coming across the fields with their lanterns. The little rural schoolhouse was packed before seven-thirty.

Two important events occurred during the eight weeks' revival in which thirty-six people were baptized. Ila preached her first sermon, and she met her future husband, Joseph Ashcraft.

The first five weeks of revival, Joe battled conviction, and he stayed home the night before his conversion to "get hold of himself." The last three weeks found him looking unto Jesus and at Sister Bill's pretty helper. Before the meeting ended, the Lord assured Joe that someday he and Ila would marry.

The next few years were busy ones for Ila as her ministry expanded and she ventured out alone. She learned early to trust God to supply her needs. If she needed something, she didn't write home; she prayed!

One hot summer she was again in Kansas. She had one dress suitable for church, and she washed it every day. While preaching one night, she reached behind her to pull her dress away from her perspiring back and tore a hole in it when it stuck to her skin. Before the next service, God supplied her with other clothing.

Joe Ashcraft had gone to California to work in 1930 and was wooing Ila with the help of the U.S. postal system. In the spring of 1933, he headed east. Ila, still unsure of God's will, entreated her mother, "Mama, Joe's going to be here right away. PRAY!"

Her mother teased, "It's too late to pray when the devil has come."

Ila may have been uncertain, but Joe wasn't. While he led testimony service in the Morris church one night, someone started the chorus "I'll Live On." They sang it rather fast and Joe, who had Ila on his mind, found himself singing, "Ila Vaughan, yes Ila Vaughan, through eternity, Ila Vaughan." He was red-faced when he returned to his pew.

April 30, 1933, after attending a fellowship meeting at Collinsville, Oklahoma, the young couple slipped away to a private residence and were married by the Reverend W. H. Lyons. This marked the beginning of a unique partnership that lasted over thirty years.

They evangelized and held pastorates in Morris, Oklahoma; Wewoka, Oklahoma; and Hot Springs, Arkansas, before they founded the United Pentecostal

Church in Okmulgee, Oklahoma, in 1951.

They shared the work of God equally, each complementing the other. His was a teaching ministry—hers was evangelistic. He handled business—she managed the home. He performed marriages and she conducted funerals. Someone said, "He marries 'em and she buries 'em."

Ila had a delightful sense of humor and would sometimes turn aside a compliment by telling something on herself. A young person, after sitting in her Sunday school class, said to her, "I wish I could have been in your class as a child. You make everything so clear."

Ila replied, "Oh, I don't know, darling. I'm not always a success. One time I taught a lesson on the treasure hid in the field. I used a ten-carat diamond as an illustration of a treasure. The little ones' eyes were big and round and I could tell they were listening, so I thought I was doing a good job. At the end of the lesson I asked the question, 'Now, what was buried in the field?' A little boy timidly raised his hand and said, 'Ah-a-a carrot.'"

Ila knew how to pray. A prayer, praise, or song was on her lips continually. Her favorite songs were "Jesus Is the One" and "I Know the Lord Will Make a Way for Me." She sang as she prepared a meal for visiting ministers and had no butter to serve and no money to buy any. She prayed, "Lord, You know it's important for us to have butter for this meal, and You are able to supply."

As they were being seated at the table, the doorbell rang. A church member brought fresh garden produce, and at the bottom of the sack was a pound of home-churned butter.

Joe relied on Ila's prayers and would sometimes slip her a hasty note regarding a need during church service.

One such note read, "I left the missionary money on the table and the door unlocked. PRAY!"

"Let her own works praise her in the gates" (Proverbs 31:31).

The door of Ila's house was open to all—saint, sinner, preacher, or evangelist—and regardless of rank, she treated all with the same hospitality. She counseled, fed, and ministered to those with a need. They were her children.

A friend of hers said, "Your secret was safe with Ila." Not only was it safe, but she carried it daily to the throne of grace until the need was received.

Ila was the first Ladies Auxiliary president for the Oklahoma-Kansas district of the United Pentecostal Church. When Sister Mary Cole, who was the international Ladies Auxiliary president at that time, introduced the Mother's Memorial program, Ila wholeheartedly promoted it in the Oklahoma-Kansas district.

In 1961 Ila was appointed International Ladies Auxiliary president at the Dallas, Texas, convention. She served in that capacity until the time of her death, February 13, 1964.

Even in death she made an impact on those around her. As she lay dying, she was speaking in tongues. The Catholic nun who was caring for her came out of her room, crying. She asked the family if Ila had studied foreign languages. They said, "No."

Then the nun said, "Surely this woman had a close contact with God."

The local funeral director, who was well-known for his quiet dignity and stoic expression and who had watched Ila comfort countless families, stood at the head of her casket with tears coursing down his face.

"Her children arise up, and call her blessed" (Proverbs 31:28).

Although not her biological children, the following ministers recall their memories of Sister Ila Ashcraft.

"I have known Sister Ila Ashcraft from my childhood. I grew up calling her Aunt Ila. She reached out to me through a tape recording when I was serving in the United States Armed Forces in Germany. Knowing she was praying for me helped sustain me through a difficult period of my life. She was a precious woman."

–Reverend C. Larry Grissom, Henryetta, Oklahoma

"I was in my early teens when the Ashcrafts came to my home church for a revival. It was the first time I had ever been in a revival where the evangelists took turns preaching. Brother Joe would preach one night and then Sister Ila. I was overwhelmed.

"It was Brother Joe's turn to preach, and both of them came early to pray. Kneeling side by side, Brother Joe was really feeling his need and was crying out to God for the anointing. Sister Ila would just groan every once in a while. Finally he stopped praying, leaned over close to Sister Ila and said, 'Come on, Ila, quit coasting and get to praying.' Of course, she told it on him and we all had a good laugh. I have long remembered that great team.

"Sister Ila Ashcraft was one of my favorite lady ministers, and she could cook about as well as she preached. Many were the happy hours we spent in their home, our home, and in the respective churches."

–Reverend C. M. Becton, Dallas, Texas

"There are so many memories. She was like a second mom to me, and I called her Aunt Ila.

"During the time of her mother's final illness, Ila had such strength of faith in the midst of suffering. Although I hated to see her hurt, I was inspired to see her rise from the depths of sorrow to face another day, to see her smile again.

"As a young evangelist, I was sometimes on the road late at night. If I happened to be in the Ashcrafts' neighborhood, I did not hesitate to knock on their door at one or two o'clock in the morning. Uncle Joe always answered the door, but when Aunt Ila heard my voice, she got out of bed and dressed. After welcoming me, she would go to the kitchen and bake biscuits and serve them to me with sorghum molasses and butter while we talked.

"She was tremendously supportive of me and my endeavors and imparted a sense of spiritual security."

–Reverend Jim Shoemake, San Jose, California

There are many more who join these to call her blessed.

Many years have passed since she left this life, yet she is still remembered not only for her works or for putting the welfare of others above her own needs and comfort, but also for the joy, happiness, and hope she shared through Christ. Hers was a full and abundant life, not materially, but spiritually. She passed this spiritual heritage on to her many "children."

by Frances Vaughan

Ila Vaughn and Willa Peters, evangelists, 1928

Brother and Sister Ashcraft around 1954

Ila and the little boy she rocked to sleep, 1957

Ila Ashcraft, 1961

CHAPTER TWO

Jennie (Seltenright) Berger

"Get out of the Book of Acts," he blurted indignantly, swinging his arm in a sweeping motion, his face exhibiting a look of pure disgust.

Jennie Berger had just asked her pastor a question pertaining to salvation. Obviously, it disturbed him to hear her refer to the Book of Acts as a basis for her question. Likewise, to hear him refer to Acts in such a contemptible manner disturbed her. "Isn't the Book of Acts in the Bible? Should we not read and study it like the rest of the Bible?" she wondered to herself.

Arising from his chair the pastor walked toward her, Bible in hand, and continued sharply, "You need to let me teach you."

"But isn't the Book of Acts true and reliable?" she questioned sincerely.

Still standing with his Bible in hand, a scowl on his face, and obviously agitated by her questions, he reiterated, "You heard what I said. Get out of the Book of Acts and come, let me teach you."

"But I don't understand!" she replied earnestly, feeling deeply the sting of his insinuation.

"Look, if you want to continue in our church, drop this Acts business. If you don't, you're not welcome. I don't want you discussing in our church what you've brought here today!" he stated bluntly.

Her face blushed faintly, and with an anguished look in her eyes, she meekly replied, "I'm sorry that this disturbs you, Pastor, but I have been reading and studying this, and I am convinced that the Book of Acts contains the truth about salvation."

Angrily, he turned and stalked out of the house, leaving her shocked at his demeanor. She found it difficult to comprehend what had just occurred. It was incredible! He had cast a shadow of doubt over the New Testament account of the early church. He indignantly threatened to dismiss her from the house of worship for believing the biblical account of the beginning of the church.

"My pastor doesn't believe in the Book of Acts!" she murmured to herself. "I wonder why?"

Previous to this encounter she had questioned the district elder of the church about baptism in the name of Jesus Christ. Very frankly he admitted it to be the truth but candidly remarked that he couldn't preach it as he would be dismissed from the church.

"Mrs. Berger, if you want to be baptized in the name of Jesus Christ," he stated, "I will do it."

"No, thanks," she replied, thinking that if he didn't have a conviction strong enough to preach what he knew to be true, she didn't want him to baptize her.

"What's this all about?" you may ask. There's a story behind it.

Bertha Mangun had just recently been baptized in the name of Jesus Christ and received the Holy Ghost. Previously a very shy, timid woman, she now became amazingly bold about her experience with God, so much so that it stirred the whole area.

Bertha was the wife of Walter, the Sunday school superintendent of the nearby Brethren church, and mother of Gerald Mangun and grandmother of Anthony, pastors of the Pentecostals of Alexandria, Louisiana.

It was the beginning of the apostolic message in that area.

In a very short time, Jennie's sister, Effie, called Bertha to sympathize with her. She thought Bertha was off her rocker but was soon convinced otherwise, and she, too, was baptized in Jesus' name and received the Holy Ghost. This brought strong discord between her and her sister. Jennie resolved to prove her wrong.

She was quite sure that her sister was in error. In discussions between them, however, her sister quoted what Jennie didn't know was in the Bible.

It was during this time that she questioned the district elder about baptism, feeling confident that he would provide her with plenty of ammunition against baptism in the name of Jesus Christ. She was utterly dismayed to hear him declare it to be in the Bible. Although not accepting it then, she did, however, consider it more seriously.

Jennie was born on July 26, 1891, in Marshall County, Indiana. She graduated from Lapaz, Indiana, high school in 1908. Her mother was a member of the Lutheran church, so as a young lady, she was confirmed in that church. Later she married Elmer Berger and they spent their married lives as farmers.

"What would happen if I believe Acts 2:38?" she thought. The question bothered her. Her sister was so happy and jubilant, seemingly thrilled beyond herself. Every time they met, the subject came up.

The encounter with her pastor was the turning point. She recognized by his demeanor that there was something he didn't want to face or that at least made him fearful. She now knew that the truth which he avoided was that which she wanted.

She was soon baptized and received the Holy Ghost. She became a fearless ambassador for Jesus Christ. She taught the plan of salvation in her home and testified about it in the neighborhood.

Jennie Berger was a strong character, being Oneness apostolic through and through. She never wavered nor compromised the truth. She believed firmly in holiness in heart and appearance.

One of the notable friends in her life was her doctor, Otis T. Bowen, of Bremen, Indiana, who later became a three-term governor of Indiana. On several occasions when she was a patient in his office, she testified to him about the message of the gospel. Later, while he was governor, in a conversation with N. A. Urshan, at that time pastor of Calvary Tabernacle in Indianapolis, Governor Bowen mentioned Jennie's testimony and sincere devotion to the Lord Jesus Christ.

Before she died in 1967, most of her children were saved. She prayed long and fervently for her husband. After her death, he came to God at age eighty-two and remained faithful until his death at ninety-eight.

Why write about this mother in Zion? Because one of her children became quite prominent in apostolic circles.

Jennie (Seltenright) Berger

First as the wife of an evangelist, then as a pastor's wife, appointed as president of the Ladies Auxiliary of the United Pentecostal Church, District of Ohio, and finally for many years the president of the Ladies Auxiliary of the UPCI, she is Vera (Berger) Kinzie.

by Fred Kinzie (son-in-law)

Jennie Berger at the age of sixty

23

CHAPTER Three

Lois Van Dyke Dyer

The new pastor of the little Pentecostal (Holy Roller) church on East Broadway in Louisville, Illinois, (population 900) was Reverend Howard Eddie Dyer. He had been baptized and received the Holy Ghost at Bethel Tabernacle in Mt. Vernon, Illinois, where Brother Ace Summers was pastor.

He was fresh out of Bible Training Center in Houston, Texas. He was a single, tall, good-looking young man of twenty-two years with glistening blond hair and sparkling, sky-blue eyes. He was full of Holy Ghost fervor and zeal and truly had a burning desire to be a soulwinner. What better place to start than Bob Bunnell's drugstore on the town square?

Lois Van Dyke had come home from Southern Illinois University in Carbondale, Illinois, to spend the summer. She was pursuing her lifelong desire to be a schoolteacher. This had been her second year of study. Her first year was spent at Illinois College, Jacksonville, Illinois. Her parents were thrilled that she was planning to return to her studies in the fall. Her father, Virgil Van Dyke, had taught school for many years.

Brother Dyer walked into the drugstore, looked behind the soda fountain, saw my mother (to be) and said to himself and to God, "She will be my first convert, and she will become my wife. Thank You, Jesus."

Mother ran with a group of four girls who had gone to school together since primary grades. They had been cheerleaders together in high school and college as well. Now they were all interested in meeting the new "Holy Roller preacher." Since Mother had already served him an ice-cream cone, she had met him; but the others had not. So they all decided to attend a church service.

The very first time Mother went, she was moved by the Spirit of the Lord. The others did not return, but she did. She attended a cottage prayer meeting the next Sunday afternoon and wonderfully received the baptism of the Holy Ghost. The members of the prayer group took her down to the Little Wabash River, where my father (to be) baptized her in the name of the Lord Jesus Christ! She was his first convert!

The next day Mother went to church to help with the cleaning. Dad found some time to talk with her.

My grandfather, knowing about the conversion, met them at the door and instructed my father never to set foot on his property again! So my dad said, "Lois, do you love Jesus? Do you love me?" Her answer to these questions was a resounding, "Yes!"

That night she packed a bag and gathered together the little money she had saved. She agreed to meet Dad downtown early Wednesday to go away with him and be married.

Dad borrowed a car from Tennis Burke, a church member, and met Mother at the appointed time and place.

They stopped at a little store on their way and bought Mother a simple, silver wedding ring for $2.25 from the money she had saved. She wore that ring until she passed away in 1997. My sister, Gayla Rigdon, wears it today.

They decided to go to Harrisburg, Illinois, where Dad's friend, Brother A. D. Van Hoose, was a pastor. When they arrived at his home, he told them he was just leaving to go to the radio station to do his daily broadcast. He told them to come along. They did, and they were married live over radio station WEBQ on August 14, 1935. Three days from soda jerk to pastor's wife!

They returned to Louisville to give themselves to the work of the Lord. They lived in a couple of rooms behind the sanctuary. After a time my grandparents grew to love my father and our family very dearly.

Early in 1936, Dad's good friend, Brother M. J. Wolff, asked my father if he would be interested in moving to Benton, Illinois, where there was a young church and some good job opportunities as well. By this time my parents were expecting their first child—me. It was the middle of the Great Depression. No one had money—especially a preacher. So they moved to Benton. Dad pastored and worked days in the railroad car shops. I, the first of eight children, was born August 5, 1936, at home. My medical bill was $3.

Mother told us that many days Dad went to work with an egg sandwich because she opened the door and found groceries without knowing where they came from. God took care of us. Mother weighed 94 pounds and Dad weighed 135 pounds because he fasted three days a week, every week, and faithfully prayed one to two hours a day.

Mother told us the story about a church member who had purchased one hundred baby chicks to raise. She planned to bring eggs and ten grown chickens as her tithe to the ministry. However, she came one day and said she was sorry but the pastor's ten chickens had died.

When I was two years old, Mother gave birth to twin girls who were stillborn. She named them Judy and Jill. The attending physician said that they were completely developed but had literally starved to death because Mother had not had proper nutrients for them. This was a very low and difficult time for my parents. Mother had prayed for and sung to her babies before they were born—even before it was the popular thing to do.

Brother Miller, and Brother N. J. Bibbs, the Indiana district superintendent, came to Illinois to meet my father.

After much prayer and discussion, my father returned to Indiana with Brother Bibbs and Brother Miller. He came home and told my mother that it was God's will to move to Hartford City, Indiana, where there was a small group of people with a building to worship in. The Millers were moving to Muncie, Indiana, to pastor. So my parents moved from "Little Egypt" to the North.

God brought tremendous revival to that church. Mother was very involved. The neighborhood opened up to them. She started ladies' prayer meetings and Ladies Auxiliary; taught Sunday school; was youth leader and church janitor; led song service; sang with Dad as he played the guitar; started and directed Vacation Bible School; and walked the streets witnessing to the community. She was constantly busy and active in the work of the Lord.

Mother told the story of their first convert in Hartford City. "Across the street from the church, Lem Gibson was working on his roof. Dad, ever bold, walked up to the house and hollered, 'Sir, do you know Jesus?' Lem came down off the roof, later came to church, and was converted with his entire family. His sons became United Pentecostal Church ministers. His wife, Helen, worked side by side with my mother for years. Mother never drove a car, so Sister Gibson took her where she needed to go."

Mother was so faithful to her God, her husband, her family, her church, her friends, and her faith. She was always positive and cheerful with a great sense of humor. She had great spiritual energy, great physical energy, great moral energy, great intellectual energy, and great peace-making energy.

Mother instilled great faith in her children, even when we were very young. One Christmas, my two-and-a-half-year-old sister, Nancy, wanted a doll buggy. Mother told her to tell Jesus about it.

Our family went to Needler's Furniture Store to check on purchasing a new bed. Mr. Needler saw Nancy and asked her what she wanted for Christmas. She told him, "Jesus is going to bring me a dolly buggy." The gentleman was moved. He called my father aside and told him to come back the next day and pick up the buggy for her!

Mother's favorite ministry was praying with people to receive the Holy Ghost. She had a very strong voice. You could usually hear her above the others, but many people were brought to speaking in tongues through her ministry. She would often say she saw the Holy Ghost in the form of a blue, hazy cloud over a person just before he began to speak with tongues. She was always at Dad's side when he baptized someone in Jesus' name.

One time a candidate was being prepared for baptism, when Mike, our brother, who was three at the time, swallowed a nickel. It lodged flat in his throat. I remember Mother praying, "In Jesus name!" I saw the nickel slide down. She went on to help with the baptism, and the woman received the Holy Ghost.

Mother loved going to Pastor and Sister Lester McFarland's farm in Lynn, Indiana. We had great dinners there with fine farm food. We would all go out in the yard and play ball. They had four teenagers, who all became involved in the ministry.

Another of Mother's great joys and gifts was entertaining "the ministry." We always had great ministers and evangelists staying with us.

One of my favorite couples in Indiana was Brother and Sister Paul Gregory. They had no children of their own; of course, I was the center of attention. He also had a big camera and a big car. He was a big man! Mother enjoyed cooking for him. He was very fond of rabbit.

One of the sisters in the church raised rabbits and gave us one. Dad brought it home. It was a beautiful white bunny with pink eyes. Dad started to kill it but couldn't. He took it back to the sister and traded it for a brown one. Mother fried it for Brother Gregory.

Mother always worked right along with Dad, never complaining. By now they had outgrown the little church. They built a new addition on the church and completely remodeled it. How wonderful to get an inside toilet! Mother and the ladies made food for the workmen each day. They also had bake sales to raise money for the project.

Now there were three children. Besides me, Nancy and Mike had joined the family.

In 1947, I went with Dad to Toledo, Ohio, for a conference where he was speaking. Brother Tommy Miller was the pastor. One of the attending ministers was Brother S. R. Hanby. He was currently the interim pastor of Christian Apostolic Church in Newark, Ohio. The founding pastor, Brother James A. Frush, had passed away a short time before. Brother Hanby talked with my dad about considering coming to Newark to pastor. This was August. By October, after much prayer and discussion, we came to visit the church. We stayed with the Hanbys (five of us and five of them) in the parsonage next door to the church. After a week, the church accepted Dad as pastor. We returned to Indiana, packed our belongings and moved to Ohio.

Our two families lived together for six weeks while the Hanbys finalized plans to move to Logan, Ohio, to start a new work. We had a great time! However, I'm sure six weeks was long enough!

Mother once again locked into her calling at home and at church. Soon there was another daughter, Gayla (Rigdon). Now there were four of us children.

However, Mother was blessed with good help from the church women and "built-in" baby-sitters. She never missed a service or an opportunity to go with Dad to visit and pray for the sick and needy.

One night during service, Sister Charlene McCreary ran up to mother (she always sat in the second row so she could lead in worship and "cheer" Dad) and dropped her newborn baby into Mother's arms. The little boy had turned blue and was not breathing. He was a tiny pree-mie. Mother notified Dad. She prayed, the church prayed, the baby coughed a few times, began crying, and was totally revived! He is still living today.

Mother had great faith. She had learned to trust God for any and all things! There were six of us children, and not one of us suffered serious illness or was ever hospi-talized. There were not even any broken bones! We just always prayed. Good thing! We had no insurance.

Mother wore many hats—literally. We always lived in parsonages that were across the street from the church or next to it. She was always running back and forth, always in a hurry!

Once when our church was hosting a district confer-ence, the ladies said, "Oh, Sister Dyer, your pink and white hat is so pretty!" She looked in the mirror and dis-covered that in her haste, she had put on two hats—one white and one pink!

Another sister, Kimberly, joined the family. Mother always said she wouldn't take a million dollars for any of her children, but neither would she give a nickel for another one. Later in life, she said that had she known her children would have been so good to her, she would have had more!

Mother was always cooking, cleaning, and given to hospitality. I'm sorry we did not keep journals or guest books. It would read like a "Who's Who of Pentecost." One of the most memorable times was when the Kinzie evangelistic party came for revival. There were five of them and six of us! We had three bedrooms and one bath-room. We got ready for church in shifts. What great times those were!

Lois Van Dyke Dyer

Then the Paslays came several times. I always wanted
to stay up after church for a "bite to eat" with the adults. I
would ask Mother to please not tell me when to leave the
table; just look at me and I would go. However, one night,
she had to "look" at me several times. I finally started up
the stairs, but not too far. She heard me and came to see
what was going on. I told her I just couldn't go to bed
because the devil kept telling me that she wanted me to
leave so they and the Paslays could do something "worldly."

In 1956 Chester and Molene Hensley came from
Texas to Newark for revival. It was glorious! Every night
people came from our city and neighboring areas to be
saved. The church was overflowing each service. People
were stretched out on the floor speaking with tongues.
Sixty-six people received the Holy Ghost and fifty-eight
were baptized! What a joy! Mother was right there working in the altar.

We had now outgrown the "old" church, and it was
time to build a new one just across the street. Dad and the
men of the church were the builders. Mother and the
ladies prepared food every day for the workers. The
ladies also had fund-raising projects with which they purchased all the seating and the carpeting. The new church
was built and dedicated.

Now it was time for another sister! However, this situation was a bit different. Mother was forty-five years old, but
God was gracious and gave her a beautiful daughter, Jamie.

I must admit I was not too excited about this event. I
was married now to Ron Newstrand, and we were expecting our first child in November of the same year. Jamie
had been born in May.

My father had preached since he was sixteen years

old. He quit high school, hitchhiked to Texas, and began preaching. He never stopped until his health began to fail. On October 7, 1970, at fifty-six years of age, he passed away. He had preached and pastored for forty years.

Mother entered a new phase of her life. She was left with two young daughters, eleven and fifteen, but she continued to work for the Lord.

On Sunday morning after Dad's funeral (attended by 125 ministers), Mother taught Dad's Bible class, and we children sang a special song. God had sustained us all. Underneath are His everlasting arms!

My husband became pastor of the church and has been for thirty-two years. Mother worked faithfully with us until her death.

She was elected Ladies Auxiliary secretary for Ohio. I was elected the president, and my husband was the district superintendent. We filled these positions for fifteen, sixteen, and fourteen years respectively.

During those years, Mother traveled with me extensively to speak for ladies' conferences, retreats, etc. One time coming home from Connecticut, I took her to downtown New York City where she had never been. She loved it but was petrified.

One day at a ladies' retreat, Mother was speaking on the platform, behind the large, solid wooden Bible stand. She felt something moving under her dress and realized that her panty hose were creeping to her ankles. She gingerly bent over during a convenient time in the message, and stepped out of them, and placed them inside the pulpit! I am sure that she retrieved them later.

In 1976 we dedicated a new church building, adjacent to the one my father had built. Brother Newstrand and the men built it in eleven months. As always, Mother was there every day with the ladies preparing lunch and dinner for the workers. She never stopped!

Mother had never had a driver's license until Dad passed away. One of the dear, patient sisters of the church, Sister Naomi Clark, taught her to drive.

She bought a car and got some new false teeth. My brother-in-law, Charlie, said, "Sister Dyer is so happy. She can now eat and run!"

One of the highlights of her ministry was the time Sister Urshan asked Mother to speak at the ministers' wives' breakfast at General Conference. Her wisdom and humor blessed us all.

It was Christmastime 1997. As was the custom, our family met for dinner, fun, fellowship, and gift exchanging at my home. There were forty-two of us. Mother had such a great day being with all her family. We always had a special time of prayer and carol singing. Mother always led us in prayer. Little did we realize it would be the last time. She was eighty-three years old. She had served God and her family for sixty-two years!

Two days later, my sister Kym went to awaken her but could not. She was asleep in the arms of Jesus!

Hundreds came to celebrate her life with us. All of her children, grandchildren, and great-grandchildren who are old enough have been baptized in Jesus' name and filled with the precious Holy Ghost. Seventeen of them sang at her celebration service. There are pastors, associate pastors, music ministers, youth ministers, church secretaries, teachers—all carrying on Mother's work!

"Her children arise up, and call her blessed" (Proverbs 31:28).

Following is my tribute I shared that night.

MY TRIBUTE

Everyone loved my mother, Sister Dyer. Sometimes I would tease her about being weary of hearing people say how wonderful she was. Not really, because that was a great joy and compliment to us, her children.

She was easy to love—always pleasant and positive with no pretense.

She had a great wit and sense of humor. She was serious about her walk with God and those things which had to do with her service to Him. But she never took life itself, with sorrow, disappointment, and heartaches, too seriously. She chose to meet head-on these times with intense prayer, much faith, and the joy of the Lord—her strength.

She knew what she believed. She lived what she believed. She taught what she believed. There was no wavering, and there were no gray areas in her life.

Mother loved her God most and foremost. She loved her church family, her biological family, and God's house.

Her children chose to love those things that she loved. What a godly example!

My mother was a lady with strong virtues, impeccable values, high morals, extreme goodness, bountiful kindness, complete righteousness, intense godliness, deep modesty, and sincere humility.

What a heritage!

by Lois Anne Dyer Newstrand (daughter)

Lois Van Dyke Dyer

Mother and me,
November, 1936

Pentecostal Church,
Hartford City, Indiana.
Dad in front with
accordion, 1939

Mother at General
Conference, 1942

Our family, 1948

Lois Dyer, 1995

CHAPTER Four

Eary Elizabeth Rineheart Dyson

In 1907 James Henry Dyson was among the first in Arkansas to receive the baptism of the Holy Ghost with the initial evidence of speaking with tongues. He was baptized in the titles, "Father, Son and Holy Ghost," by Brother Howard A. Goss. Brother Dyson had the Holy Ghost for seventy-five years at the time of his death.

This new Pentecostal doctrine spread through Arkansas, and Henry's mother and father, James and Bammer Dyson, were among the known "heretics" who worshiped at the Church of God at Woodson, Arkansas.

Henry fell in love with Eary Elizabeth Rinehart, and Pastor McDonnell married them on November 5, 1916, at Orion Missionary Baptist Church.

After losing their beloved three-year-old daughter, Mary Katherine, in 1920, they decided to take their eighteen-month-old son, James Lafayette, and move from the Woodson-Redfield area to Little Rock.

Henry sought out the Pentecostals. He remembered the wonderful beginnings that started with Brother and

Sister W. L. Stallones at Seventh and Cross Streets, over a grocery store. Then Brother and Sister Ralph Cook became pastors. When the Pentecostals sought for a location for the first Southern Bible Conference in Little Rock in 1922, they rented an Episcopal church on the corner of Fifth and Victory Streets, just two blocks from the Arkansas State Capitol Building. This church later became the First Pentecostal Church.

When Brother and Sister Cook felt led of God to return to Boston, Brother and Sister G. H. Brown, who were already there, became the new pastor and wife.

Eary fervently wanted an experience like her husband's, so she prayed and sought after God; but the baptism of the Holy Ghost did not come easily. She continued to take her young sons, Lafayette and Charles Ray, to the Emmanuel Baptist Church in Little Rock while her husband went the Pentecostal way.

Around 1929, after another son, John Henry, and daughter, Margie Elizabeth, were born, the Dysons moved from Little Rock to a small community called Geyer Springs, eight long miles from Fifth and Victory.

Eary continued to seek God and said, "God, if the Pentecostal way is real, let me feel it, too." In her own words she said, "I shook for three days under the anointing." That same year she was filled with the Holy Ghost and was baptized in Jesus' name by Pastor G. H. Brown. In later years, she became the Sunday school teacher for the ladies' Bible class. Her holy life was very effective through her witness and in praying for and with her family, friends, and neighbors.

Henry was baptized in Jesus' name in a Sunday morning service by Brother Brown in 1933, while Brother

Howard Goss was there ministering. Brother Goss had now been preaching the Jesus Name message for many years. Brother Dyson also served in many offices of the church, including Sunday school superintendent from 1927 to 1957.

Another son, Paul David, and another daughter, Marilyn Ruth, were added to this wonderful Christian family. They were raised in the Pentecostal doctrine at Fifth and Victory, and Brother G. H. Brown baptized them all in Jesus' name. They were taught that they were overshadowed by the mighty power of God and were protected from all evil forces. Also by leaning on the strong shoulders of the Lord and believing and trusting the God who never fails, they could come through trials or burdens victoriously every time. Prayer and fasting were the keys.

About 1962, the Dysons moved their membership to the Apostolic Church of Jesus Christ, North Little Rock. Brother George L. Glass, Jr., was their pastor. Brother Dyson taught the Bible class for about ten years.

In 1979, the senior Dysons moved from Geyer Springs Road to Sherwood in North Little Rock. Due to Brother Dyson's failing health and Sister Dyson's constant loving care for him, they were not able to attend services as they had always done before.

During this time their children cared for their needs with love and compassion that had been ingrained in their upbringing. Brother Mervyn Miller, their son-in-law, was their pastor. He, along with the apostolic church members, went to encourage the Dysons almost daily. Because prayer was part of every visit, they always left lifted in spirit by the blessed presence of the Lord.

Reverend Charles R. Dyson, Lafayette, John Paul, and

Marilyn (wife of Brother Miller) all attended the apostolic church in North Little Rock. During this time Margie was the wife of the general secretary of the United Pentecostal Church, Reverend C. M. Becton. He served in that capacity for many years.

* * * * *

My Mother's Philosophy of Life

My mother, Eary E. Dyson, was of German descent. She had four general philosophies of life that she taught to her children.

The First: God and Church

My mother never neglected going to church. She and my father both had the new-birth experience. In everything, she always considered, "If it's the Lord's will." Not only did we go to every service at church, but we had a "church" atmosphere in our home with family prayers, Bible reading, and the whole family studying the Sunday school lesson together on Saturday night. As a result, all six children experienced repentance, the baptism of the Holy Ghost, and Jesus Name baptism. One son became a United Pentecostal Church minister and the other three sons ministered in UPC churches in singing, teaching, and lay ministry.

The Second: School and Education

My mother believed in education! She allowed no excuse for missing school. The oldest son went through grammar school, junior high, and high school without missing a day for twelve years! The others only missed when a childhood disease did not cooperate with the school holidays. We were always told that we were not sick, we just thought we were! All six children finished high school and some went on for further education.

The Third: Work and Employment

Mother taught her children the proper relationship between employee and employer. She advocated going early to work (before clock-in time) and staying late if needed. Father taught his four sons the furniture trade as he was a foreman in a furniture factory for over thirty years. They all became successful Christian businessmen and owned their own factories and upholstery businesses. Mother taught her two daughters by example how to become homemakers and also soulwinners. They both married preachers.

The Fourth: Play and Recreation

The sons took care of the livestock and were outdoorsmen, enjoying hunting, fishing, and family sports. Play always came after study and home chores. The daughters' recreation and play was churning, ironing flat pieces, and cookie making. This was my mother's concept of play! But, of course, we always participated in family sports of ball playing and indoor and outdoor games.

* * * * *

More Memories

Many years ago, a happy young family with three rambunctious boys, ages five, seven, and nine, and a six-month-old baby girl, mother and father moved from the capital city of Arkansas to the country. From their "secret garden" consisting of five acres of brush and rocks, a spot was cleared and four comfortable rooms were erected to house this adventurous group.

From farm to factory by way of rocky lanes and curvy roads to crowded streets, the breadwinner traveled twenty miles six days a week.

An old-fashioned Baptist circuit preacher had married this couple twelve years prior to the eventful move, and one day he paid them an unexpected visit. Surveying the fenced-in area with large posts on either side of the cattle guard, he suddenly suggested, "Dyke, why don't you call this place 'Rocky Comfort'?" And for many years the affectionately named, unpainted plank with painted letters hung high above the entrance gate.

Two more children blessed the family in later years. The youngest served with her husband and family for fourteen years as a United Pentecostal missionary. One son was a United Pentecostal Church minister. I was the six-month-old baby girl who grew up to marry a United Pentecostal minister.

Fifty years of living at Rocky Comfort, Geyer Springs, Arkansas, holds a reservoir of fond memories. After Mother was filled with the Holy Ghost, she knew exactly what had happened to her good Baptist mother. She had fallen into a trance at one of the protracted summer revivals at the Orion Baptist Church. They finally carried her to the wagon and stretched her out on a blanket. She jabbered something that they could not understand the entire journey home and on into the night. Mother began to put the pieces of the puzzle together and discovered why her mother would allow her daughter to marry a young Pentecostal man.

Her dear Henry had received the Holy Ghost at the tender age of twelve at a revival meeting at Redfield,

Arkansas, where the Holy Ghost was first poured out in the early 1900s.

The Arkansas campground of the United Pentecostal Church is located near the spot of the outpouring, according to my father's oldest sister, who lived near the campground for many years. She lived to be 103 years of age and was full of the Holy Ghost when she passed away.

Mother spread the fruit of the Spirit to all of her family, neighbors, and faraway friends. A weekly prayer band met in her home. Oh, such praying and travailing, especially during World War II, as she had two sons overseas. The prayer band from the church and the prayer meetings at the church services were powerful. Everyone came home from the war whose name was on the special prayer board in the church.

Many times during the night I would awaken to Mother's praying for the boys in battle, and we would hear a few weeks later by mail how that one of the sons had almost become a fatality. When they returned home, Mother would get their letters that she had received and compare their miracles, as she had written down the time and date of her intercessory prayer.

Her best friend for over fifty years was Christine Becton. I never referred to her as a mother-in-law. She was always my other mother or my husband's mother. She too had a son overseas, and this bonded them even closer.

Nearly every Saturday they were at one or the other homes having meals, fellowship, and studying the Sunday school lesson. They always ended their times of fellowship with prayer. Another family, the L. J. Riffes, met with them most of the time. Most of them were Sunday school teachers, and they took teaching mighty seriously, checking to see that the Word backed everything that they taught.

Mother was very sensitive to the Spirit, and this caused her to be burdened for a neighbor a mile away. She went to the neighbor's house and prayed for her baby who was sick with a high fever. The baby was healed. Her closest neighbor, Mrs. Watson, a devout Methodist, received the Holy Ghost in our home. She had to move away shortly after receiving the Holy Ghost, but Mother saw to it that she was established in a United Pentecostal Church in Lonoke, Arkansas. Mrs. Watson remained faithful until her death.

Rocky Comfort was the place where accidents and miracles occurred. One of the boys, Charles, was accidentally shot in the eye with a BB gun. Upon examining Charles, the doctor said that he would be blind. Mother and Daddy would not accept this, so they prayed all night and God healed him. Several years later when applying for employment at the Missouri Pacific Railroad Company, he passed the eye test with 20/20 vision. To God be the glory!

A short time later when he was called for a physical required to enter the United States Army, he was classified 4D because of something they saw in his eye, which kept him out of the service. This was a continuation of the miracle that even though he had been shot in the eye, he still had perfect vision. To my knowledge, he never wore glasses.

God knew that he would be needed at home to assist with the Dyson family affairs. But even more than that, he would be greatly used in the church while many men were absent.

When John was very young, he was playing and ran through a barbed wire fence. He got a six-inch cut from the corner of his mouth across his face. After Mother prayed fervently, the wound stopped bleeding and began to heal. No stitches were taken and yet there was no scar. God performed another miracle.

Lafayette was known as a free bleeder. He had a wisdom tooth pulled and bled profusely for hours. I remember Mother praying on this wise, "God, You gave him this blood because he needed it; now I want You to take charge here and stop the bleeding." It stopped instantly. Another miracle was wrought.

Reverend and Mrs. G. H. Brown, our pastor and his wife, were in our house all night long on two different occasions. Paul (Buzz) fell from a tree, knocking him unconscious. Our pastor and his wife and our parents prayed until he regained consciousness, another healing mercy.

The other occasion was when I was in first grade and had missed school for days with a high fever from an infected mastoid gland, which caused great pain in my ears. My parents had used all the home remedies but to no avail. Our family doctor left our home shaking his head and saying, "Tonight will tell the tale. She has a fifty-fifty chance." There were no miracle drugs at that time. Our pastor and his wife, along with my parents, prayed through the night. I had not eaten for days and was dehydrated from the high fever. Around 4 A.M., I sat up in bed and asked for water and a hamburger. Dad called the doctor and asked if I could eat this. The doctor said, "Yes." I ate, and I was healed. Another miracle had taken place. I was back in school in two days.

We didn't just stay in bed and pray; we always got up and knelt on the cold floor when we would get a phone call for prayer for someone. This was what our parents called "gaining the victory through prayer."

Mother had a few unusual sayings and quotes:

1. Never take advantage of anyone's generosity.
2. Only tell jokes that can be told in Sunday school.
3. Beauty is in posture, so stand erect.
4. Praise makes good men better and bad men worse.
5. To love and be loved is like being warmed by the sun on both sides.
6. Peach trees are good for two things: savory fruit and slender switches.

The ending of a life fully spent as a child of God has many rewards. You really can't say that we lost our mother because when you know where someone is, she is not lost.

One day my husband and I drove from St. Louis to Little Rock, Arkansas. We stopped by to check on my mother and dad and, as always, had prayer before leaving. We then drove on to southern Arkansas and checked on my husband's parents. The next day we drove to Oklahoma for a marriage retreat.

We received a call from my sister saying that Mother had taken ill after we left the day before. Marilyn took Mother to the doctor, and he ordered bed rest for her for two or three days and gave her some heart medicine. She felt great after resting and taking the medicine, and several friends came by to see her.

A family reunion was planned for the following Saturday

at Mother's house. We left Oklahoma that Saturday morning and arrived in the afternoon. Sure enough, all the family seemed to be there. Some were on the porch and some were standing in the yard. Marilyn came to the car and informed us that Mother had passed away that morning. Mother was the one having the reunion; but rather than a family reunion, she was having a reunion with the Lord. She died of congestive heart failure.

It was a privilege to help dress her and fix her hair as a corpse. She was beautiful even in death. The funeral was three days later at Rest Hills Funeral Home and Cemetery—very appropriate for a weary pioneer to be in "Rest Hills." Over the past few months, she had told us how tired she was caring for our father, but she was not tired of him.

Throughout their sixty-seven years of marriage and the past four years of our dad being bedfast, they really were close. In fact, when Marilyn went into his bedroom and told our father about Mother's passing away, he said, "Pray for the Lord to take me too. I have no reason to live." We told him how much we needed him and he replied, "You don't need me and I don't need you. Just pray for what I asked you to."

My brothers took our father in his pajamas and robe to a private viewing of our mother. Being in a wheelchair, he was asked if he would like to be raised up to a level to kiss her. He said, "No, I kissed her goodnight just a few hours before she died. I just want to run my hands through her hair."

You see, the very last time that I saw Mother alive, less than a week before, I told her how good her hair looked and asked who had fixed it. She said, "I did, and your

49

father really liked it." He paid her a nice compliment about her hair, and she twirled around like a new bride. My father loved Mother's long hair, and even though she had four sisters that kept their hair cut very short, she never gave in to their ridiculing. Oh, they claimed to be Christians, but not Pentecostal Christians.

Reverend George Glass, Jr., preached my mother's funeral from Isaiah 38. Hezekiah was sick, and the prophet told him he would die. He did not know that he would get well and have fifteen years added to his life. Hezekiah said, "I have cut off like a weaver my life." Throughout the message Brother Glass referred to Mother as "the little weaver." As the story goes, the weavers would cut off their threads at the end of the day. Weavers, in those days, were more like slaves. The weaver would cut off the cloth, leaving more to be finished the next day.

The lamb gave the wool, the master gave the fabric, and we do the weaving. In the Master's absence is the best test of our fidelity. Have we goofed, erred, or have we completed the pattern? The weaver was rewarded more for coarse wool than fine wool. Our pioneers had some wild or coarse wool to work with.

Everyone in the ministry in our family has at one or more times used the title of "The Little Weaver" and some of the thoughts when preaching a funeral of a loved one whom he pastored, or was requested to speak for a person of the same integrity as my mother. Usually, it had to be a person of great significance for him to use a portion of the message.

A choir made up of the grandchildren sang a medley of Mother's favorite songs at her funeral. A granddaughter sang "He Does All Things Well."

Eary Elizabeth Rineheart Dyson

To an Old Cemetery

Rest quietly, you pioneers, though no flags fly.
You are remembered, though no bugles blow.
No day is set aside to say we honor you.
Yet in the hearts of many, you receive the honor due.
'Tis true, we did bestow no medal—
(Hard work receives but few.)
And yet when hauling grain today,
I said a silent prayer of thanks to all of you.
Thanks for your vision, courage, patience and
        trusting hearts.
And grant, dear Lord, that I may do my part
To pass down through the years a bit of hard-
        garnered heritage.
Rest quietly beneath the oak, you pioneer,
Though no flags fly to mark the passing years.

by Margie Dyson Becton (daughter)

Eary Reinhart, age 17, and Henry Dyson, age 21; early dating years

Brother and Sister Dyson, 1975

Eary Dyson, 1975 St. Louis, Missouri

Margie Becton, daughter, and Eary Dyson, 1980 Nashville, Tennessee

CHAPTER Five

Ethel Elizabeth Goss

Ethel Wright's father, Simcoe Wright, was born and lived near Rome, Georgia, with his father and mother. The War between the States was over, and most of Georgia was devastated: no crops, no food, nothing for the Wright family to live on. Since Simcoe (Coe) was the oldest, he found a wagon and a team of horses. His father had been killed in the war, so Simcoe put his mother and several younger children on an open wagon with everything they owned. Across Alabama and Mississippi, they trekked all the way to Benton, Arkansas. Simcoe later married Annie Samuels. By the time Ethel was born, he had become a well-respected businessman and a prosperous blacksmith.

He often increased his income by taking wild horses off the Western plains and, to use his terms, "gentled" them. Then he sold them to families who wanted horses dependable enough for their children. He was well-known for his integrity and sobriety and also his impatience with anything corrupt. He was never interested in anything religious but had many sayings that he quoted.

When Ethel began to preach years later, she had a difficult time sorting out many of those wise sayings that her father quoted, not realizing that they were not actual Bible verses. Here are two I remember:

Every tub must stand on its own bottom.

He tempers the wind to the shorn lamb.

While still living in Benton, Ethel had her first awareness of God. One day as a toddler of two walking out in the tall grass of the back garden, she was talking out loud to someone. Wondering to whom she was talking, her mother came to the back door and called to her, "Ethel, who are you talking to?" Ethel remembered the incident very clearly. Her two-year-old mind realized suddenly that there was no visible person there, so she replied to her mother, "No one, Mama."

She knew, though, that she and the Lord had been carrying on a conversation. As she answered her mother denying this, she felt the warm feeling go away, leaving her cold and uncomfortable. From then on, she always knew that there was a strong connection between her and God.

Ethel's mother, Annie Wright, was a respected leader in Malvern, a committed Baptist, and president of the Women's Missionary Society. After Simcoe died, the family was left with very little. But Annie learned to trust the Lord in every aspect of their lives, and she went on to raise ten healthy, talented children to adulthood, sustained and provided for by her godly wisdom and trust in the Lord.

Ethel was two years old when the family moved from Benton to Malvern, Arkansas. Later when Ethel was a young woman, she became ill with five diseases that were incurable at that time. Her parents felt that she would get better if she went north to stay a few months in the Ozark mountains. While she was in Yelleville she began attending local revival meetings. The following experience became a major turning point in her life.

While she was staying in a hotel, she began attending the revival meetings and felt a deep hunger to know more of God. She often spent her days reading and praying for that purpose. One day while she was praying in her hotel room, she was overwhelmed by the presence of God. She felt literally saturated with God's presence. Hour after hour in His presence, she lost all understanding of anything around her, not caring what she was saying or praying. She only knew that she was overcome by the love of God and realized that she was being physically healed, cleansed in mind and spirit, and was brought into a secure, deep relationship with the Lord Jesus Christ.

It seemed to her that even the pure white bed linen she was touching in her bedroom was not clean enough for her to touch, so pure and white did she feel! Hours later, when she left her room to go out into the street, she felt free and light. On returning to Malvern, she was restored to perfect health.

Another revival meeting was in progress in Malvern, but since it was not sponsored by her Baptist church, it was of little interest to her. None of her Baptist friends were attending, so she paid little attention to it. However, she was invited one evening and so attended with several of her girlfriends. Ethel had heard rumors that the evangelist, Howard Goss, was hypnotizing people into doing strange things. Her impression during the meeting was that his "little green eyes" wouldn't be able to hypnotize anyone!

There was a call from the platform at the close of the service for "all the Christians to come forward and help in the altar." Ethel felt that she would be dishonest if she did not respond, so she went forward and knelt at the altar. While there she began to worship and pray, again aware of the same presence of the Lord that she had experienced before she came back from the mountains.

Among the evangelists that Howard Goss was a part of at that time, there was a firm belief that one had to be "sanctified" before he would receive the experience of speaking in tongues, which was called the baptism of the Holy Ghost.

When Brother Goss overheard Ethel at the altar speaking in fluent tongues, speaking in a language other than English, he was very puzzled. Since he had never seen her before in any of his own meetings, and since he also knew that his was the first Holy Ghost revival that had been held in that part of the country, he was perplexed at what he was hearing.

After the meeting he asked Ethel, "When were you sanctified?" Being a Baptist who believed that she was already pure and sanctified through the new birth, and not believing in the Methodist doctrine of sanctification, she bristled at the question. She replied that she was a Baptist and did not believe she needed a separate experience of sanctification.

Brother Goss later realized that here was evidence of God doing something beyond his present doctrinal understanding and the accepted teaching of that time. (Later the doctrine of requiring a sanctification experience prior to the infilling of the Holy Spirit fell away as unscriptural.)

Ethel realized that the same experience she had received in the mountains was exactly what others in the new move of God were experiencing, so she joined the revival. Some time later when a team of workers were being readied to go out and hold meetings in new towns, Ethel felt she was being led to join them. She became well-known as an accomplished evangelist, pianist, and soloist and was on the field for several years before she later married Howard Goss, her former pastor.

Ethel's father was so opposed to all "this religious stuff" that he told Ethel he would never give her one cent of support if she left home to go out with the team. The whole team of workers lived by faith, fully confident in the Lord's ability to supply their every need.

One time Ethel was to take a train at an appointed time and was without her fare even though she had just closed a revival meeting in that town the night before. Apparently no offering had been taken. She went through all the right motions, got to the station, and was standing at the ticket window asking for her ticket—but without a cent to her name! As the stationmaster asked for the fare, someone behind her laid down an amount of money that more than paid for the ticket. She opened her purse to put in her ticket, and the same hand scooped all the change right into her open purse.

(According to the chapter entitled "A Love Story" in the book *The Winds of God*, Brother Goss traveled frequently. Unfortunately, his young wife, Millicent, had died after the birth of their daughter in 1909. Apparently Brother Goss drowned his grief in the work of the Lord. Friends of his were concerned that he remarry, and they felt God had showed them the right woman. Meanwhile Ethel Wright was not too interested in matrimony but certainly wanted God's will in her life. She was shocked when

God showed her "a choice young man," Brother Howard A. Goss! Earlier Howard had had a somewhat similar experience. In 1911, he found he had one weekend in August unexpectedly free, so he telegraphed Ethel where she was stationed in Galena and asked her to meet him in Eureka Springs and marry him on Monday.

She conferred with a senior worker, Sister Arthur, who said, "Go! Hasn't anyone showed you what the Lord showed Sister Miller?" When she talked to Sister Miller, the lady handed Ethel her train fare, as well as money for the hotel and other incidentals. Another woman contributed her bridal outfit. She filled her regular Sunday appointments, and then took the midnight train to Eureka Springs. Howard arrived the next day.

The hotel owner provided hothouse blossoms for a bridal bouquet, and the Gosses were married in the double parlors of the Chatangua Hotel. Ethel wrote in her book, "The Galena saints thought that we would be so perfectly suited for the Lord's work that they were happy, and so were we. Time proved them right.")

They had only one day available for a wedding and just one night in a hotel for a honeymoon. The next day they each returned to their separate posts miles from each other, until they were able to rearrange their schedules and start their new life together. None of their family members were present at the wedding as both of their fathers disowned them when they went into the ministry. Fortunately, their mothers didn't; Daddy's mother was converted in the very same revival as Daddy. His father, though, died an atheist as far as anyone knew. Ethel was not at home when her father died, but her mother's relationship with her never wavered.

(Editor's note: According to the unpublished notes of S. C. McClain as written in the book, *United We Stand*, by A. L. Clanton, page 13, Howard A. Goss was converted and baptized in Jesus' name in Galena in 1903. In 1915, Goss was again baptized in Jesus' name, by Brother H. G. Rodgers because he had not fully understood the significance of his earlier baptism.)

Ruth Nortje, their daughter, says, "Regarding when Ethel was baptized in Jesus' name, it would be most likely to assume that Brother Goss, her pastor and husband, baptized her following his own baptism by Brother H. G. Rodgers."

In *The Winds of God* Ethel described the hard work and travels of the young evangelists. From one town to another they carried the gospel, preaching in tents, storefronts, and any sort of vacant building they could obtain. In the book, *United We Stand*, by A. L. Clanton, one gets a glimpse of young organizations forming, and Howard A. Goss is usually in some place of leadership.

What does all this traveling from place to place entail for a young bride who became the mother of six children? Ruth, their daughter describes one incident that seemed to have had lasting effects.

Before I was in my teens, once while we were traveling in a car with Daddy, Mother asked Daddy to stop the car. Not realizing that the car had not completely stopped, she stepped out and went flying into a ditch, rolling over and over. Never one to make a big fuss over any physical problems or pain, she recovered herself and was able to get back into the car with Daddy's help.

Quite a while after, though, she discovered that she had permanently injured herself. From ear to ear there was a permanent indentation at the base of her skull. Even years later, when I would give her a head massage, I could lay half my finger into the cleft running from ear to ear. Of course, this affected her in a number of ways that were not really known or understood by those outside the family. Her nerves became sensitive and any continual noise was hard on her. It also affected her sleeping.

My father snored, and together they raised three boys, who also began snoring as they grew up. This fact became quite a trial to my mother. Having a musician's ear, her hearing was very acute. Quiet resignation was her way of life, so I seldom heard her complain as she tried various ways of handling life. We children were trained to be quiet and considerate of Mother, and Daddy always made allowances for her. Slamming doors or yelling through the house was a no-no. Many times she would work herself to a standstill as she cooked meals or gardened.

Mother was an accomplished pianist with a photographic memory of any music score she saw. She could copy any dress pattern or design an original if necessary. She made almost all the clothes we six children wore, even trousers for my three brothers. All the family learned to become good cooks.

Mother and Daddy loved people, and entertaining people in our home became normal. One year we counted that for eleven months, our family of eight entertained one or more guests at our table each day. The church and our apartment above it was one block off a major artery into the city, Danforth Avenue. So because of Daddy's esteem among missionaries and ministers around the world, visitors seldom came to Toronto without dropping in.

Ethel Elizabeth Goss

The doors of the church and our apartment were never locked, so it was not strange to have visitors arriving late at night to slip into the guest room without waking the family. They knew they were always welcome. It happened once, though, that two ministers who were not very friendly with each other woke up one morning and found that they had actually been "sleeping with the enemy."

Mother had the ability to prepare a whole meal from seemingly nothing. Mother, always innovative, could make any meal taste delicious, which was great training for the ministry and living by faith in later years.

I can never remember a time when we six children sat down to the table without being served a nourishing and delicious meal. Roast lamb with mint sauce and pineapple upside-down cake were family favorites. Daddy also cooked and was renowned for his Mexican chili con carne, mainly because it was hot, hot, hot!

Regarding Mother's basic philosophy and attitude toward life: I (Ruth Goss) can only say that in every aspect of her life, she depended on the Lord to lead her, strengthen her, and give her wisdom and leading.

For example, when I was about six years old, a member of the church in Toronto made a gift of a small summer cottage to the family. It was located about twelve miles from Picton, a small town between Toronto and Montreal where Daddy and Mother had pastored in 1919-20.

Each summer, though, Mother had a big problem. Since our summer holidays in Ontario were two and a half months long, there was a lot of planning involved in getting the family organized for the big move to the cottage. Mother had difficulty in getting Daddy to give her a fixed date for the trip. He never seemed to want to set a date until the Monday morning that we were to leave. Getting laundry washed and ironed for six children, clothes packed, etc., and being ready for a Monday morning trip took days of planning and preparation. Daddy never seemed to understand a mother's need, since he could pack and take a train to California at an hour's notice.

Looking back, I think that this was a little game that they played between them. Daddy never liked a lot of fuss, and Mother liked to plan ahead and organize so that everything could be smooth and peaceful. Nothing was really said about how Mother managed it all, but I think Daddy realized that she had bluffed him someway by always being so prepared.

If Daddy needed to hear from the Lord on big issues, Mother was always the one whose prayers and counsel he sought out. They would go to the bedroom, shut the door and talk quietly for several hours, their voices going back and forth. Finally we would hear them praying. When they opened the door, the issue was resolved and they would be at peace, ready to move forward.

Concerning Mother and her Bible, how can a person tell the value of Bible study in the life of another? What I do know is that one seldom went into Mother's sitting room next to her bedroom without seeing her big Bible lying open on the large desk in front of her. She studied with several translations, but the King James Version was her foundational reference. Quite often I refer to two of her Bibles that I have today in my study: the Berkeley Version of the New Testament and the New English Bible/New Testament. All the verses in her Bibles that she had underlined in red ink, are very important and precious to me.

Mother's talents in music and speaking were well-known throughout the organization. She wrote numerous songs:

For example:

> Once in the dawn of Creation's morn,
> The Saviour walked among men;
> Down the green aisles of Eden so fair,
> He walked and He talked with them there.

Chorus

> Oh, is the Saviour with you tonight?
> Does He walk close by your side?
> Is He the One Who is dearer to you
> Than all the world beside?

Another song was "I Fell in Love with the Nazarene." Her alto voice was rich, and the listeners knew she was singing from her heart.

During the years of their pastoring in Toronto, each Sunday Daddy preached in the morning and Mother preached an evangelistic message at night. The auditorium seated about five hundred, and it was usually full to hear her preach. There was a large prayer room in the basement, and many seekers would be there by the close of the service. After singing a solo and preaching an evangelistic sermon, though, Mother would be exhausted. Some people are energized by the anointing of the Lord, but Mother would be exhausted by it. By the next Sunday, however, she would have another message ready.

My mother lived completely dependent on her Lord. He was always her first "port of call" when faced with any difficulty or decision. If she lost or misplaced anything in the house, she would walk through the rooms, quietly saying, "Lord, show me where that is." Without any doubt, we knew that Mother was definitely closely linked to the Lord.

As children, our first thought in any kind of trouble was to find Mother, knowing that she would handle the situation either with wisdom or prayer or both. She never put guilt or condemnation on us because she knew that we knew what was expected of us.

She always needed to conserve her energy and was frequently troubled by heart fibrillation and irregularities. She seldom felt she needed the care of doctors as she continually depended on the Lord to keep her going, and He always did!

In the mid-forties Evangeline, now married and living in Brockville, Ontario, became very ill after an operation. Daddy, Mother, and I were living in St. Louis at the time, and Mother felt she needed to be nearer to Evangeline, so we made plans to move permanently to Picton.

That meant, though, that the four-room summer cottage needed to be remodeled and winterized. This was in the late 1940s when building supplies were very scarce all over Canada after the end of World War II. It certainly was not the time to build anything.

However the Lord supplied everything that was needed and more. It took about eleven months to complete the remodeling. The Lord helped Mother at every turn, supplying all the lumber, nails, the heating system, and the labor.

Evangeline recovered, and Gosswood Lodge became the family's permanent home. (The joke was that Goss would lodge there whenever he could!) Joseph was now living in Houston, David in Detroit, and Daniel in Manila, Philippines. They were able to come and visit us now; at last there was plenty of room for all of us. Mother was the planner and director of the entire project. Daddy was away most of the time, still traveling and taking care of the organizational needs of the United Pentecostal Church.

Mother enjoyed the home, the large rooms, the big front-room fireplace, her own suite of rooms where she could be quiet for her writing and studying, and especially the large garden. Mrs. Goss's garden later became a local attraction for many people who would take a Sunday drive past the home, just to see her display of blue delphinium (sometimes six feet tall) banked on each side by dozens of pink peonies and petunias in the long border beside the house.

Mother would work in the garden every time she had the strength. It was her delight. We also developed a vegetable garden in the fertile virgin soil that kept us fully supplied, with enough left over to sell at the roadside.

The fact that she would need several days rest after one of her gardening days, seemed to be normal as she enjoyed it so much.

One day, though, as she was getting dressed to receive visitors, her heart gave out, and she lay back on her bed and was peacefully united with the Lord she had loved and served for seventy-six years.

by Ruth Goss Nortje (daughter)

Ethel Goss and children at the Picton Train Station, 1920

Ethel Goss

CHAPTER SIX

Maria Kate Weedman Hardwick

In the late 1800s John Weedman and his family migrated from French Lick, Indiana, to Tennessee. John was the youngest child as well as the only son in the family with several sisters: Sarah, Mattie, Mag, and Lucy. The Weedmans joined the Fleshiers on a flatboat and floated down the Ohio to the Mississippi and on to Dyer County, Tennessee. Mr. Fleshier brought a sawmill with them which he planned for John to operate.

They settled in a small community called Lenox. John met and married Annie Myra Fuqua. Her younger half-brother, Alison Kirk, married Carrie Fleshier. Mr. Fleshier bought hundreds of acres of property surrounding Lenox in Dyer County. John also bought two small farms and built a homeplace in the small village of Finley, south of Lenox. An excellent carpenter, John Weedman built many of the homes in Finley.

John and Annie had a daughter named May and two sons, Barney and Norman. In 1905 their last child was born, a little girl named Maria Kate.

When the boys got big enough to help on the farm, John set them to chopping cotton. Soon he scolded the boys. "You're chopping down the cotton as well as the weeds!" Annie watched the boys, then said, "John, those boys can't see well enough to tell the difference between cotton and weeds." After testing they found that Annie was right, so John sent the two boys to Nashville to the Tennessee School for the Blind. May went along to take care of the boys. In addition to Braille, they learned how to make brooms and weave cane bottoms for chairs.

One summer while the boys were home on vacation, they took meningitis and Barney died. Norman recovered and went back to the School for the Blind for another year. May met and married Will Earl.

Meanwhile James McDonald Hardwick and his brothers, Walter and Frank, sons of a Methodist preacher, Eli S. Hardwick, had migrated from Metropolis, Illinois, to Helouise, a small village on the Mississippi River in Dyer County, Tennessee. He worked in the tall timber as a timber cruiser, estimating the amount of timber on the land. A Jewish friend advised him, "Buy land, Jim Hardwick. Put your money in land. It's the best investment you can make!"

So the young man, who had met and married Rosie Belle Joslin, began to buy land. He finally owned almost a thousand acres and built a nice house on the banks of the Mississippi for his growing family. They had ten children who lived to be grown, as well as some who died as children. They included George, Lawson, Gladys, Anna, Mack, Albert, Walter, Faye, Cecil and Rosa Margaret.

Almost every spring the Mississippi River went on a rampage and flooded the countryside. The houses were built on stilts to accommodate the floods. One year the water was lapping so high that it was almost to the door. A steamboat came steaming up the river, hugging the bank. "The waves from that steamboat will wash our house off its stilts!" Jim cried as he reached for his rifle and shot out the windows in the captain's cabin of the boat. That caught the captain's attention! He turned the ship back toward the middle of the river. Tough times call for a father's decisive action.

The Hardwick's daughter, Gladys, became sick and died and was buried in a small cemetery in Helouise, but the raging floods washed the cemetery away. Jim decided that the Hardwicks needed a home further from the river, so he got John Weedman to build him a house just around the corner from the Weedman home in Finley, ten miles in from the river.

One day while Lawson Hardwick was getting a haircut, Maria and her mother passed by the barbershop. "There's one pretty girl you won't be able to date, Lawson," said Chic Holt, the barber. "Betcha I can," the Hardwick boy responded to the challenge. Before long he was courting Maria.

Maria was a top student at the Finley high school where she studied Latin, math, English and domestic science. Her father, who played the fiddle, also paid for piano lessons for Maria. "If you'll keep on with your music, when you finish high school, I'll send you to the conservatory in St. Louis," he promised. But the Hardwick boy won out, and Brother E. J. Douglas performed their wedding ceremony in August 1923.

Church played a big part in Annie Weedman's life, as well as Maria's. In 1916 Brother Joiner and Brother Mills came to Finley preaching about the Holy Ghost. Annie Weedman and her daughters, May and Maria; Sister Victor Michell and her daughter, Cora L.; and Sister Verdun and her daughter, Mollie, were among the first to accept the Pentecostal message. Later Brother E. J. Douglas, along with Brother Ralph Earl Glasgow, came preaching the oneness of God and Jesus Name baptism.

One man, Brother Bobo, joined with the women. John Weedman built a church for them next to his home.

The small village of about five hundred people had started with a community church that later became the Church of Christ; then came a Methodist and a Baptist church. Summer revivals were the town's main events, and Maria's family attended them all. When there was a death in the village, the school would sometimes dismiss so that everyone could go to the funeral. Finley folks cared for one another.

The Pentecostal church was a well-built white frame building with homemade pews, a potbellied stove, a pulpit, a large altar, and a pump organ. Later the small congregation instituted a penny march and paid for an ebony black piano. There was an outside toilet. Baptisms were conducted in either the Obion or Mississippi River.

Maria's first daughter, Mary Martha, was born in 1924, and about two years later, a little girl, Gloria Faye, was born. Lawson, along with some friends and cousins, left Finley to find work in the automobile industry in Detroit. Maria and her girls stayed with her folks.

One day Maria went to Dyersburg to shop. When she returned, Annie told her, "Maria, the baby is puny. You go on to prayer meeting to play the piano, and I'll stay here with the girls." When Maria got home from church, her concerned mother said, "Maria, go ask Mr. Hardwick to go get Dr. Luther to come. This baby is real sick." Dr. Luther was the stepson of Aunt Mattie, almost like family. He stayed all night, but just before dawn, the nine-month-old baby died. A telegram brought Lawson home, and the young grief-stricken couple faced their first major hardship.

Later Lawson took his wife and little girl, Mary Martha, to Flint where he worked in the auto plant until the 1929 crash. That year another baby girl, Norma Jane, was born.

When Lawson was laid off work at the automobile plant, he decided, "Let's go farm on Papa's Helouise farm." Maria missed her mother and her church, but she took her piano to the farm with her. Later, when the Weedmans' house burned, she was glad she had her piano with her in Helouise. John Weedman soon rebuilt his home.

After a year or so, Lawson got a job in the Dyersburg Cotton Mill, so they moved back to a small two-room house that belonged to her brother, located right in front of the church. Here their first son, Lawson Hugh Hardwick, Jr., was born.

When Lawson was still a toddler, Maria got a job in the cotton mill also. She made $7 a week and Lawson made $10, a great salary during the Great Depression, which was in full force in the thirties. For $2 a week and board, Maria hired a "nurse" to watch after the children. The nurse slept in the front room downstairs, and Lawson and Maria and the children slept in the attic. But the baby hardly slept at all. After many sleepless nights, they discovered that the "nurse" gave the baby a drug, paregoric, which made him sleep all day.

"Maria, you all move in here with us," Annie Weedman insisted. "I'll take care of the baby." So they did. Later, when the little boy was about four, he took "summer complaint" and almost died. Mary Martha remembered how his eyes were set back in his head. Dr. Luther did his best. The church prayed, the whole town prayed. Brother Glasgow drove forty miles from Jackson, Tennessee, to pray for Maria's boy. Slowly he began to mend, and Maria learned more than ever the power of prayer.

The Pentecostal church (often referred to as the Holiness church) grew slowly under the good leadership of Brother Glasgow. Annie Martha Earl, Maria's niece, had a job at Woolworth's, and her tithes together with Maria's helped pay Brother Glasgow's gas bill. He lived in Jackson but drove down each weekend for service. The women met on Wednesday nights for prayer meeting. Brother Glasgow ate Sunday dinner at Maria's or Sister Michell's. There were no restaurants or motels in Finley. Sister Michell, Sister Verdun, and Sister Pritchett gave what they could and held the church together during the Depression. Mary Martha finished grammar school in 1938, but before she went to the new consolidated high school in Dyersburg, she was baptized along with some cousins in the Mississippi River. Later that summer she received the Holy Ghost.

About this time other preachers from Jackson and Bemis visited the church. They included E. E. McNatt, J. W. Wallace, and W. M. Greer. Maria, Annie Martha, Rebecca Edwards, and Leota Batton formed a ladies' quartet and even rode the ferry across the Mississippi River to sing on Brother T. Richard Reed's radio broadcast, "The Blessed Old Bible Hour," in Corning, Arkansas. The family back in Tennessee listened to the program on their new Philco radio.

Brother Glasgow decided to take a leave of absence and left the church with Brother E. E. McNatt from Bemis. James McDonald Hardwick divided his estate, and Lawson's share was about $3,000. John Weedman gave Maria a lot on the street behind his home, and they built a new four-bedroom house.

Brother McNatt rented the Weedman house and, for the first time, the Pentecostal church had a resident pastor. Brother A. D. Gurley came and preached a tent revival. New people began attending. The congregation grew. Later Brother McNatt took a church in Memphis on Fourth and Keel. Brother W. M. Greer took the Finley church, but he kept his job at the Bemis cotton mill.

About this time J. O. Wallace came to Finley with his father, Brother J. W. Wallace. He and Mary Martha began to correspond. He had finished Draughn's Business College in Memphis, but due to the draft, he decided to go back to Bemis. In 1940, he went with his father to found West Nashville Pentecostal Church (now called First United Pentecostal Church). This was the first Pentecostal church east of the Tennessee River in the state. Soon, however, J. O. was drafted into the army, but letters from Finley continued to flow.

While he was stationed at Santa Barbara, he planned a furlough to attend Mary Martha's high school graduation. While there he and Mary Martha became engaged and planned to marry that summer. But the Japanese shelled the California coast and all furloughs were canceled. So Lawson quit his job at the cotton mill and took his daughter to California to marry that soldier.

In 1943 in God's providence, J. O. was stationed at Thayer General Hospital in Nashville just a few miles from the West Nashville Pentecostal Church, which worshiped in a basement on 51st and Delaware. Attendance was about seventy, and out of this number, seventeen boys were in the United States Army. Mary and J. O. began Sunday afternoon prayer meetings for those boys, and not one was even injured, although one was in the Battle of the Bulge. The church was growing, but there was no Pentecostal pianist. Brother Wallace hired a woman, Mrs. Willis, to play. Mary began to pray, and soon she suggested that her dad could find carpenter work in Nashville. He came and liked the city, so the Hardwicks moved to Nashville in 1943.

Maria became the pianist, and before long a teacher, Grady Moore, was hired. Many of the young people began to learn to play instruments: guitar, mandolin, and ukelele. Maria taught piano. She was also appointed as leader of the Ladies Auxiliary.

During the war, building materials were hard to find, but after the war, J. W. Wallace planned to build the sanctuary. It was completed and dedicated in 1948.

Several ministers came to hold revivals. One team was the Rexie Wilcox/C. M. Becton team. "Oh, good," Maria thought. "I'll take some lessons from Brother Becton to improve my piano playing, Pentecostal style." Her training had always been classical music, and she had difficulty playing by ear. Later two young men from the Pentecostal Bible Institute came to help in meetings. One was Ted Black, also a great pianist. So Maria and her daughter both took lessons from him.

When the sanctuary was completed, J. W. Wallace asked Maria to buy a new piano to replace the ancient upright they had used in the basement. She went to town to shop but came back and asked Brother Wallace, "Could we just buy a spinet piano instead of a baby grand? Then we could raise some more money and buy a Hammond organ!"

This was a huge step of faith, since no other Pentecostal church in the state had an organ at that time.

Brother Wallace, always a music lover, quickly gave his consent. The Ladies Auxiliary began to raise money. They had bake sales, garage sales, and other fund-raising projects. Maria always led the way. Some murmured a bit about having church suppers where they donated the food and then paid to eat, but the money came in dollar by dollar.

Maria took lessons on the organ and loved its beautiful tones. Family, church, music—these were her passions.

Her children grew up and married and the grandchildren began to arrive. Maria always was anxious when any of them became sick. She knew that a baby could die overnight. But she always remembered the prayer of faith that had touched her oldest son.

After the war J. W. Wallace remembered the vision he had of churches in the north, east, south and west part of Nashville. J. O. and Mary had started the Goodlettsville church while he was still in uniform, and it was now pastored by Brother W. T. Scott. He and Mary went to Bob Jones College and later to Tupelo, Mississippi, where they taught Bible school for a year.

In 1949 J. W. heard of a small church for sale in the

Woodbine area. He and J. O. looked it over and arranged to buy it for just $1400. J. O. and Mary moved to Woodbine and began to pastor that church, with just fourteen members including Maria's seventeen-year-old son, Lawson, whom Grandpa Weedman had nicknamed Barney in honor of his blind son who had died.

J. W. Wallace held the first revival, and Eugene and Verna Ferguson came in. Later Brother McNatt held a tent revival. Claude and Eloise Malan from the Bible school stayed one summer to help. Door-to-door visitation brought in Sister Reavis, her daughter, and mother. Rexie Wilcox came and held a revival. Slowly the church grew.

About this time J. O. was elected as secretary of the Tennessee District. Then the superintendent, Brother W. M. Greer, asked J. O. to come to his large church in Bemis, Tennessee, to assist him as well as serve the district as secretary.

"What can we do with the Woodbine church?" he asked his father, who was presbyter for this area.

"Leave it with Brother Hardwick and I'll watch over it," Brother Wallace planned. After Maria's son had married the Carson's oldest daughter, Montelle, and had begun to pastor the Woodbine group, Maria and Lawson decided to move to Woodbine to assist their son in the church there. She had taught the young Robbins girl, Vadean, to play the piano and organ so "Deanie" could fill her place in music in West Nashville.

Montelle's parents, Noble and Maggie Carson, also moved to Woodbine to assist the young couple.

When Brother E. J. Douglas came to hold a revival in Woodbine, he went fishing with Lawson, Sr., and convinced him that he loved him, but that God loved him even more. So Maria's husband, for whom she and her children had prayed for many years, gave his heart to God, was baptized in Jesus' name by his son, then later received the Holy Ghost! What rejoicing! What a great reward for years of living for God, serving Him faithfully with her music and leadership talents, and seeing her children, third-generation Pentecostals, serving God. God does answer prayer. A faithful wife can live to see her companion find God.

When J. W. grew older, his son, J. O., resigned his position at the United Pentecostal Church Incorporated, where he was publishing house manager, came home, and assisted his father in his declining years. In the duplex parsonage basement, Mary began a day-care center with her four children. Before long, she asked Maria to assist her.

Later when J. O. and Mary moved to Oak Ridge to pastor, Maria took over as director. She met the requirements to have the center licensed by the state, one of the first to do so in Tennessee. Every morning she conducted a daily Bible lesson; God blessed and the center outgrew the basement.

Later, when J. O. was elected International Sunday School Director, they moved back to Nashville. The West Nashville Kindergarten moved to 5106 Knob Road in a brand-new building with four nice classrooms and an apartment upstairs for the Wallaces. Maria drove each morning from Woodbine to teach a class of four-year-olds. At their annual class day, her children were able to quote the Lord's Prayer and the twenty-third psalm. Usually in the fall there was a waiting list to get a place in the West Nashville Kindergarten and Nursery, which accommodated over one hundred students. Maria was the star teacher.

In 1975 at age seventy, Maria retired from teaching four-year-olds, but she continued an active role in church.

One day Mary called her mother. "Whatcha doin'?" she asked.

"Well, I just baked seventeen pumpkin pies for the church Thanksgiving dinner," Maria answered.

My mother was a Proverbs 31 woman. At her funeral her former piano teacher, Brother C. M. Becton, sent a lovely floral arrangement designed as a treble clef in memory of her dedicated years to music in the churches. Her old pastor, Ralph Glasgow, comforted us saying, "Today, Sister Maria has graduated. She's at the head of her class!"

Dad was brokenhearted, and for a while, we didn't know how he would make it, but Maria had left him two freezers of food plus a pantry of canned goods. So the next summer he planted a garden and canned some tomatoes.

Godly parents—what a treasure!

by Mary Hardwick Wallace (daughter)

Maria Kate Weedman Hardwick

Lawson and Maria with all the grandchildren, 1956

Maria Hardwick,
sister May Jarrett, and
mother Annie Weedman

Lawson and Maria Hardwick,
1976

CHAPTER Seven

Fern Lewis Hassell

Fern made a bargain with God. If He would save one of her sons-in-law and call him to preach, she would give up half her life.

"I was put to the test. God allowed me to have cancer and a fibroid tumor. The devil told me I would soon be gone, but I did not back down from my promise. God healed me. Praise His name!"

Fern's testimony declares Hebrews 11:6 is a reality in her life: "But without faith it is impossible to please him: for he that cometh to God must believe that he is, and that he is a rewarder of them that diligently seek him."

As God saved Lot because of Abraham's faith, He rewarded Fern's faith. All five of her sons-in-law are saved, and more than one are called to preach the gospel.

Before her healing in 1953, Fern started writing a ledger to her children. "Oh, children, I want to live so close to God that my life will be a burning testimony. When you were little children around my feet, I thought I couldn't take one more step, but with God all things are possible. He has helped me so many times when no one else could. When you take one step, God takes two."

The big steps of faith Fern made as an adult were the results of tiny steps taught to her as a child. As a descendant of Meriweather Lewis, explorer in the Lewis and Clark Expedition, her natural heritage is as significant as her spiritual heritage.

"Between the Lewises and their in-laws, they owned just about everything for miles around. They were rich in spirit, too. Through the early influence, the family has produced many Protestant ministers, most of them Baptist," reports the *Lewis Family History Book*.

The Lewis family members were originally French Huguenots. As France was predominantly Catholic, this group of Protestants became the center of political and religious quarrels in the 1500s and the 1600s.

The Huguenots believed the teachings of John Calvin and were members of the Reformed Church. The Catholic government gave them the name "Huguenots" and persecuted them.

After a law was issued granting the Huguenots freedom of worship in seventy-five towns, three brothers, William, Samuel, and John, fled to England. As craft workers and textile workers, they played a large part in building up the English textile industry. While crossing the English Channel, they changed their original name of Louis to Lewis. Eventually they migrated to America.

According to the *Lewis Family History Book*, "Daniel Lewis, Fern's great-grandfather, and his family traveled up from Alabama to Missouri in 1828 looking for a place to settle. On their way up, they stopped briefly to visit Daniel Boone and his family. Ferrying the Mississippi River, Daniel

Lewis, his wife, and three sons landed at the foot of Locust Street in St. Louis, Missouri. Not finding a suitable place for a crop in St. Louis, they went on to Herculaneum, Missouri, stayed there for a while, and then moved west.

"They came to the little Meramec River in Franklin County and followed it upstream until they arrived at a tiny community called Lonedell, not far from St. Clair, Missouri. It looked like the hills of Tennessee, where they had lived originally before they tried Alabama, so they stopped there."

William Perry Lewis, son of Daniel Lewis, died near Lonedell at the home of his youngest son, Simon, on his old homestead where he had lived for almost sixty-five years. Simon Lewis was Fern's father. On this homestead in 1908, three months before her grandfather's death, Fern was born.

Fern lived with her mother and father, two older sisters, Josephine and Evelyn, and a brother and sister from her mother's first marriage.

"Dad had two children from a previous marriage. It was a family of his kids, her kids and their kids," she said.

Simon Lewis was a horse trader and breeder. "He had a large farm where he raised pigs, cows, geese, sheep, and of course, his prize horses. He would go to Kentucky, buy thoroughbred 'bluegrass' horses, and break them for race horses. He had a black stallion he bred mares with."

Evelyn was partial to the black stallion. When Simon announced that he intended to sell that horse, she devised a way to keep him. She and Fern hid in the bushes near where they were trying out the horses. As the horse came near, they scared the horse, hoping it would buck the rider off so he would not want to buy it. Their plan failed;

the stallion was sold. However, Simon purchased an organ with the money from the sale.

"My dad was a strict Christian. He didn't know anything about Pentecost, but he was all for it, except the baptism. He allowed no cards, dancing, or worldly music in his home," Fern stated.

One day after he bought the organ, he came in from the field and caught Evelyn playing "Turkey in the Straw" and "Little Brown Jug." He walked up to her and said, "A-a-ah, if that's the kind of music you are going to play, I'll sell the organ." He never raised his voice, but that was the last of the worldly music.

After the supper dishes were done each evening, Simon called all the children and Fern's mother into the living room for Bible reading and prayer. "That was every night, not just once in a while," Fern recalls. "We were Baptists, but my parents loved the Lord and taught us to respect Him and His Word."

Going to visit Grandpa and Grandma Miller, Fern's mother's parents, was a joy for the Lewis children. Grandma Miller made homemade bread and served slices with real butter while the bread was still hot. When they butchered their own meat, they cured it by salting and smoking it with hickory chips.

Grandma Miller was sick one day, so Fern's mother decided to visit her. The girls begged to go with her, but she wouldn't let them. "You must stay here with Aunt Lydie," she told them. (Aunt Lydie was Simon's invalid sister who lived with Fern's family.)

"No," the girls protested. "We don't want to stay with Aunt Lydie. If we have to, we are going to have chicken for dinner."

"Well, you could have had chicken for dinner, but since you told me you were, now you're not," she informed them as she went out the door.

The girls decided to have chicken anyway. Fern caught the chicken and Evelyn held its feet. After losing a few badly clipped feathers, the chicken decided he had better things to do and hurried off. Shelling more corn, the girls caught another chicken and stretched it out. After several attempts to cut his head off with the ax, they talked Aunt Lydie into being their accomplice and finishing the crime for them. The girls had a fine chicken dinner and were pleased with themselves, until Mother came home.

Fern's mother kept vegetables to be stored, salt brine pickles, and sauerkraut in barrels under the house in the cellar. Simon made a long trough and filled it with cool water to keep the milk and butter from spoiling. When it thundered, however, the milk clabbered, so Fern's mother made cottage cheese. She heated the clabbered milk until it was warm, put it in cheesecloth, and hung it on the clothesline to drip dry. When she took it down, she put salt and sweet cream in it.

"Daddy made a wooden frame with cheesecloth tacked over it to dry apples and peaches. Mom put a white sheet on the flat roof of an outside building, put the fruit on it, and set the frame over the sheet and fruit so bugs or flies could not get to the fruit. They brought the fruit in at night and put it out the next morning after the sun was up," Fern recalled.

Simon made what he called an "apple pit." He dug a hole in the ground, lined it so water could not get to it, and then put in straw, apples, more straw, and more apples until the pit was full. Covering the apples with more straw, he mounded dirt on the top of the pit. When his family wanted apples in the winter, he took a pick and broke a hole in the dirt. He reached in, got the apples he wanted, and covered it back up again.

By the house, Fern and Evelyn played on flat rocks and picked blackberries. Sometimes they got in the garden. Their mother didn't want them in the garden, so she picked up tomato worms and scared them out rather than whipping them. She couldn't whip them when their old dog, Ring, was around. He protected them from anything, even their mother. They used to pick up sticks and take Ring rabbit hunting. They didn't catch any rabbits, but they had lots of fun.

Fern and Evelyn were inseparable in their younger years. Josephine, who was older, liked to "mother" them, but they didn't like her "bossing." They stayed out of her and their mother's sight as much as possible.

On the farm, the old gander liked to chase the little girls. Fern wasn't afraid of him, but he knew Evelyn wasn't so brave. He chased her to the top of the woodpile every chance he got.

The girls got tired of the gander's egotistical attitude and decided to put a stop to it. Fern caught him by the neck, Evelyn got his feet, and they escorted him to the cellar. Their mother's milk cooler was the perfect spot to conduct a baptismal service. They dunked him. "Had enough?" they asked, as they brought him out of the water. The poor goose was in no position to answer, so they dunked him several more times. "Had enough?" they finally asked.

The goose had, as they realized too late. Determined

to dispose of the body as quickly as possible, they ran to the wide creek. They pitched the goose into the creek, and he went floating down the stream without a chance to repent of his tormenting the little girls.

The girls had plenty of chances, however, to think about their crime. They crossed that creek every day as they walked two and a half miles to school. They used foot logs to cross the creek, but when it rained, their mother came for them with a horse. She swam the horse across the stream and brought the girls over one by one.

Three years before his death in 1917, Fern's dad went blind. Every morning after he got up and put on his overalls, he called Fern to hook his suspenders. She knew he could manage by himself, but it was her job, and she loved helping him. He rewarded her with a big hug, and she took him by the hand and led him around the farm.

Simon Lewis's death didn't end her love for her dad. The Bible teaches us to "train up a child in the way he should go: and when he is old, he will not depart from it" (Proverbs 22:6). Simon didn't live long enough to find the truth that Fern found, but what he knew, he taught his children. His teachings and prayers never left her.

"Mom remarried after a year. We lived on the farm for a couple of years until the drought came and we had to move in with Dad's brother, Uncle Dave Lewis. After several years, we moved to St. Louis, Missouri. I was fifteen when I met the most handsome man of my life, James Herbert Hassell," Fern remembered.

Fern found work at the St. Louis Car Factory as a seamstress. Even back then a person had to be sixteen to get a job in a factory. Fern's father had taught her that it was wrong to lie. She couldn't lie even to get work, but she figured out a way around it. Taking a piece of paper, she wrote the number 16 on it, put it in her shoe and walked gracefully in for the interview. When they asked her how old she was, she said, "Well, I'm over 16."

Fern stated, "It was in this factory that I met James. I was a seamstress for the big cushioned seats they used to put in the trains back then. James was an upholsterer. I had to go through his department to get to mine. One day he whistled at me. Naturally I turned around and looked. He curled his finger at me and motioned for me to come over and speak to him.

"When I got there, he asked me, 'How about a date Sunday?' I answered, 'Oh, maybe.' Mother had told me not to say 'yes' the first time, just 'maybe.'

"'I don't want a maybe,' he said. 'I want a know-so.' So I just said, 'Okay.'"

Their first date that Sunday was going to a church meeting. It was a Baptist church where James's friend asked him to go. Neither Fern nor James was saved at the time, but the seeds were planted in their hearts.

James's family moved to Memphis, so he moved with them and got a job. Fern and James were engaged and wrote letters back and forth. While in Memphis, James repented at a Baptist church. God told him that He had a work for him to do with a "higher power."

James came back to St. Louis to see Fern, and later his parents moved back also. As Fern, James, and James's dad were walking down the street one day, they found a Full-Gospel mission at 1414 North Grand Avenue. It was a storefront building used for a dance hall as well as church services. A big sign on the door said, "Dancing every night." Tacked underneath were the words "Full-

Gospel Mission." Indeed it was dancing every night, but not the same as that indicated by the sign on the door.

Pentecost was new then, and people came out of curiosity to see the "new kind of magic." "Spells" were cast on people when they were touched by "one of them" and people were known to go into "trances" for hours. Policemen were called occasionally by people who believed that someone in a "trance" was dead.

Fern and James returned to that church many times after their first visit. Brother B. H. Hite was the pastor of the church. He was a big man and Brother Hite excited the children when he shouted, but no one was allowed to laugh. He had a rule in his church: Boys and girls were not allowed to sit together. "Most people didn't know that we were going together," Fern said.

Grandma Miller was an "old-timey" lady. One night she went to church with Fern and James and had a "shouting spell." Instead of taking the streetcar home, as they usually did, James called a taxi. They didn't realize it was God's way of protecting them.

Fern's stepdad didn't understand this new Pentecostal experience, and he wanted nothing to do with this fellow, James Hassell, either. He decided it was time to put a stop to all the foolishness. Going down to the train station, he waited behind some upright railroad ties for them to come back. God sent Fern's stepbrother to intervene for them, however, while James whisked them home another way.

Fern and James were married at her mother's home by Brother B. H. Hite in 1926. Then they moved to Memphis where James had his job.

"To this union was born a baby girl on October 2, 1927. We almost lost you, Sweetheart," she wrote in her ledger to her oldest daughter. "Mama had a kidney problem and lay a long time with fever over 103 degrees. James called the doctor, and he put me in the hospital. I was no better, so Brother Graham and some praying saints came and God answered prayer. When you came to live with us, dear, we praised God for a sweet little bundle of love sent from heaven." Betty Jo was eight months old when they moved back to St. Louis.

"At Brother Hite's church in St. Louis, Daddy promised God that he would preach. I saw what the Lord did for him and couldn't deny what I saw, so it put a hunger for God in my heart. But I didn't repent then. I watched. There was such a change in James's life. He stopped smoking cigarettes and didn't want to dance or go to the show anymore. I couldn't understand it, but I told him that if it was wrong for him, it would be wrong for me. Finally I gave God my heart and promised I would work for Him," Fern stated.

Brother Hite moved his church to Cass Avenue. James was his young people's leader. One night the young people were practicing for the Christmas play when a gang of boys came and started making noise. James told them to be quiet. They left but waited in the covered entrance to the church. When Fern, James, and the baby came out, they made threatening remarks as they passed. Every night after practice, the rowdy boys did this.

One day Betty got pneumonia, so Fern stayed home with her. The next night the leader of the gang came up to the platform where James was and asked him about his wife and baby. He told him, and before they stopped talking, the man asked how to be saved. James baptized him and all of his gang in Jesus' name.

Fern Lewis Hassell

Another entry in Fern's ledger stated, "God added another little girl to the family. Her name is Doris Marie, and how I love her. Honey, Mom had to take you to church in red houseshoes someone threw away, but God blessed me for it. I remember one time when you woke up at night and begged for something to eat. I was in someone else's home and said, 'Honey, Mama hasn't got anything to give you.' How my old heart ached when you said, 'Mom, I love you.'

"A third little girl came to live at our house, and we called her Edith Pearl. She was born December 12, 1932. What a sweet thing she was and she looked like her daddy. I almost lost you before you were born. I held onto chairs to fix your older sisters something to eat. You see, dear, Daddy was preaching and was gone lots of times. Sometimes, I didn't have much to cook, but God let me keep you and that is worth everything to me. I love you so much."

The Lord told James to go to Gasconade, Missouri. He told God he would go if He would make the way. They got ready and went to the train station. As they stood around, someone came up to them with the money for the train fare. That was another answer to prayer.

Two years later, the Hassells moved to Evansville, Indiana, and then thirty miles farther in the country to a small town called Griffin.

Grandma Fetcher, an older saint in the church, was a prayer warrior. At a church dinner, she fried hamburgers. One lady in the church had a husband with a drinking problem. He was always around when it came time to eat. Grandma Fetcher said to everyone, "Look at this. He is so drunk he won't know if he has a hamburger or not." She got two slices of bread and put them together. He was so happy to get something to eat, he never knew the difference.

On the way home on Sunday nights, Brother Hassell picked up stragglers along the road too drunk to get home. One fellow was a regular Sunday night hitchhiker. One night the hitchhiker was not there, so they drove on home. Having no electricity, James went in first with long matches to light the Aladdin lamp. It lit the front rooms but not the bedrooms. Fern carried the baby to the bedroom to lay her down. She tried to go around the bed in the dark, but two big black boots blocked her way.

"Honey, did you leave your boots on the bed?" she asked, coming back into the living room.

"Of course not," he answered and went to investigate. He found not only boots but a whole body lying on their bed. The Sunday night hitchhiker had found his way to their home and was sound asleep.

The neighbors and friends were like one big, happy family; most of them came to church. Even sinners made a habit of going to Sunday school and church. It didn't take much to get people "happy" in those days. When Brother Hassell accidently brushed the side of his pants and one of his long matches lit, the people were too busy enjoying his "blessing" to notice the smoke coming from his pants pocket.

There was no need for "priming" with lots of choruses and reminders of "Let's all raise our hands and praise the Lord." One sister sitting on a cracked pew, pinching herself, and rising up with a little squeal was enough to get the whole church shouting.

Fern continued writing in her ledger. "Now a fourth

little fellow came to live with me. A boy this time. We named him after his daddy, James Herbert. Was I ever proud of this little angel! But when you were two weeks old, son, you took the whooping cough. For six weeks, I thought God was going to take you from me. I had waited so long and prayed so hard for God to give me a son; one to call me Mama.

"Honey, I didn't have any money to buy clothes for you. A month before you arrived, a lady lost her baby and she gave me its clothes for you.

"The fifth bundle of love came to our house on September 1, 1938. We named her Jeannette. God bless her. She is a blessing to me. Jenny, dear, Mama was in bed two months before you came to live with me. I couldn't eat much, and what I ate, I didn't want. Our house burned before you came, and it took everything to get started. All I had left was your daddy, the children God loaned me, and one diaper on the clothesline outside. But Jesus was good to spare you all to me. Baby, I pray you will always stay close to Jesus.

"My husband is one of many having a rough road to trod, but may I, Lord, hand him a clean white sheet to rest upon. Have I added a heavy load to carry on this rugged road? Have I helped him when he grew weary and sat down to rest, or have I passed by and handed him another package to carry? Jesus knows we grow weary and our burdens are hard to bear, but He promised never to leave us and every burden to share."

On February 5, 1946, God blessed the Hassells with a set of twin girls.

"Brenda Lou is my little preacher, and Carolyn Sue would make a great worker for the Lord in music and song.

I am hoping to raise them, but if I don't, take good care of them and raise them in church for me. Love, Mom."

All of the Hassell girls helped in church work and in the entertaining of visiting ministers. A minister who liked to rock came for supper one evening. They had a big cane-bottomed rocking chair. One of the girls took the cane-bottom out of the chair and stacked big pillows on the chair covering the hole. After supper, the minister decided to relax in the rocking chair. He sat down, way down, so far down his feet went straight up.

"Fern was always putting the girls up to 'meanness,'" James said with a chuckle. He should know. He was the subject of most of their "meanness." They waited until he was asleep; then they quietly sewed him up in the sheets with just his head sticking out the top. Once in his more blissful nap times, they tied his big toe to the bedpost with the twine that came off the meat wrappers then yelled, "Fire!" He thought he had it made one day when he got up only to find the ends of his pants sewed up.

While at Cambria, Jeannette called Fern to come to stay with her. She was having her first child and was scared. Fern said she would pack her suitcase. Before she left, Doris called. She was having surgery and wanted Fern to stay with her girls. She told Doris that she would have to call her back.

Fern went to the kitchen, washed her dishes, and prayed. "God, they're both mine; I can't make the choice." A sweet voice spoke and said, "Go to Doris. I'll take care of Jeannette."

After Doris came home from the hospital, Fern's brother-in-law came to take her to Jeannette. The voice said, "Go home."

"But you have been so worried about Jeannette. Why?" Her brother-in-law was upset.

Fern went home, cooked dinner, and packed the twins' clothes. They left to go to Mt. Carmel, Illinois, where Jeannette lived. By two o'clock the next morning, James was in Mt. Carmel Hospital on the second floor. The next day Jeannette was admitted to the third floor. Fern was able to be with both of them when they needed her because she trusted God's voice.

James took another church at Buckner, Illinois. He suffered a heart attack, however, and was unable to continue. He and Fern bought a small home in Tamaroa, Illinois, close to one of their daughters. After James had another bad attack, he had a pacemaker put in. Fern's heart, too, has its stubborn times, but her determination is just as stubborn.

When the Spirit of the Lord moves in a life, it makes us forget our afflictions. The anointing of the Lord is worth everything. Helping others see the way brings satisfaction. To Fern, helping others is the mode of her life. Whether it is her grandchildren or others, her delight is in the Lord.

"I have children, dear Lord, who are traveling this long lonesome road. Some of their feet are bleeding from the stones that have been laid in this road. Please, I pray, dear Jesus, bind up their poor souls, and give a double portion, as Elisha of old," Fern has prayed.

One summer Fern's grandchildren and her daughter's family took her back to her old homeplace near St. Clair, Missouri. While having a picnic lunch by the church across from her family cemetery, the pastor came and let Fern go inside to view the church. Her grandfather,

William Perry Lewis, deeded the ground where the church and cemetery are located.

The pastor said they had the original deed with his name signed to it. He invited Fern back to their 100th anniversary service.

"The first family reunion was held June 16, Father's Day, 1957, 129 years after Daniel Lewis and his family came to Franklin County, Missouri. It was held at the Oak Grove church about ten miles from St. Clair. It sits on a hilltop and all you can see for miles are wooded hills and shaded valleys. The church was originally built in 1885, mostly by Lewises. Across the dirt road from the church is the Oak Grove Cemetery," reports the *Lewis Family History Book*.

It was getting late as we traveled down the road to view the old homeplace. In the distance we saw a lean-to shanty, which is all that was left of the house. Standing in the middle of a field with weeds grown up around it, it was not inviting in the gathering dusk. But in her mind, Fern was not seeing the same thing as the rest of us saw.

Looking over the weeds and rattlesnakes, she saw two little girls playing "horses" on the saplings, waiting for Willy Mearl, the mailman, in the first car that they had ever seen.

But when we went to the cemetery, I knew why she came. Although many Lewises are buried in that grave-yard, she was only interested in one—her dad's. She searched diligently until she found it under the big oak tree. The writing was faded, but she knew that epitaph by heart. As her heart grew misty, I knew her mind was not on death.

A dark-haired man was watching patiently with eyes

not blinded anymore. His strong arms are opened wide to receive her when she takes that last step through the gate.

"That's my baby; God bless my baby," he calls as her tears are erased. "I've come to lead you to the Savior and show you our brand-new 'homeplace.'"

Fern and James still reside in their small home in Tamaroa, Illinois, close to their daughter, Sue. Their oldest daughter, Betty Jo, has been living with them since her husband passed away. When they are able, they attend church at Brother McKinnis's in DuQuoin, Illinois.

by Debbie Farrar (granddaughter by marriage)

*Fern Lewis
(Hassell) and
nephew Burton
Montigue*

*Herb and Fern Hassell with their two oldest daughters, Betty Jo and
Doris Marie at Gasconade, Missouri*

Fern Lewis Hassell

Herb and Fern with Betty, Edith, Doris, and Richard

Sue, Brenda, Jeanette, Edith, Fern and Herb Hassell, Richard, Doris and Betty

99

Herb and Fern Hasell

Fern Hassell, age 95, 2003

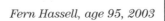

CHAPTER Eight

Lillian Gladys Gibbs Hedges

My parents, Lois Lindsey and Minnie Adams Gibbs, native Grundy County Tennesseans, moved to Logan, Illinois, so that my coal miner father could work there in the mines. Their first child, a boy, was born dead. Three and a half years later, after my parents had been married seven years, I was born on July 19, 1920. They named me Lillian Gladys.

When I was four, while Dad worked in the mines, he was hit with an electric wire behind his right ear, which blinded him. His blindness didn't last too long, but as a result they moved back to Lockhart in Grundy County, Tennessee. I had a brother, Chris Nelson, seventeen months younger than I. Later another brother, Edwin Rowlett, arrived.

I started to school two miles from our house at Sweeton Hill. I finished fourth grade there, and fifth grade at Coalmont, Tennessee.

We never went to Sunday school or church, but I had a fear of God and asked my mother such spiritual questions as "Who made us?" My mother would answer me. Four years before I was born, Mama had repented and been baptized in Jesus' name by a minister named Samuel R. Burrow. Mama received the Holy Ghost, and Dad repented and was baptized but never received the Holy Ghost. They loved to dance and lived in the fast lane. Mama played the five-stringed banjo and the fiddle for dances. She told me about her experience with the Lord, but her lifestyle was ungodly. I'd find a place alone and try to pray, but without a church home, I couldn't get far with my praying.

We moved to Sanders Crossing, and I walked two miles to Tracy City to attend the Shook school in the sixth through the eighth grades. Once a week all the classes went to the auditorium for convocation. In the eighth grade, our class was in charge of the devotion. They asked me to read two or three verses from the Bible. I was so shy that I lost my voice! I was terribly embarrassed!

While in the seventh grade, I sat in front of my teacher's desk. He was also the principal. One afternoon, he asked, "How many of you go to Sunday school?" Everyone in the class but me lifted their hands. I dropped my head. The principal, Eugene Williams, saw my embarrassment. Later he called me out in the hall and said, "Lillian, we've got a new preacher, Paul W. Travis, at the First Baptist Church. I want you to come and be with us Sunday."

Mama and Daddy were separated by this time. On Saturday I had to wash our clothes on a rub board in a tub, then iron them with a iron heated on the stove. But my brother, Nelson, and I got ready and went to church that Sunday to "get the teacher off my back." The preacher's wife was my Sunday school teacher. She impressed me, so we kept going. She even invited me to go with them to their district conference at Murfreesboro. While there, she talked with me about giving me music lessons. I accepted! "If you will come on Saturday and clean house, wash, iron, baby-sit or whatever I need, then I will give you thirty-minute piano and voice lessons."

Since God had dealt with me as a five-year-old, I was very interested in church and soon joined that church. In the meantime, two Jehovah's Witnesses came by with their literature. We didn't buy their books, but I begged Daddy to buy me a hardback four-by-seven-inch Bible for only forty-five cents. This was the first Bible in our household. I began to read. I read through Ruth, then the Lord impressed me to read through all four Gospels—Matthew, Mark, Luke and John. Then came Acts 1 and Acts 2. I was really stirred.

Since I was out of school for summer vacation, I worked at the preacher's house. One day after we had finished lunch and were eating dessert, I said, "Brother Travis, I've been reading the Bible, and I read yesterday in the second chapter of Acts about the Holy Ghost. Tell me about it."

"Lillian, I don't know anything about it, and I don't want to discuss it," he replied.

A few days later, our neighbor, Bailey Nunley, and his sister asked me to go with them to Tracy City to a brush arbor meeting. I cooked a good meal and even made a cake for our supper. When Daddy got home from the mines, I asked him to let my brother Nelson and me go to the meeting. He answered, "No." Quietly I washed the dishes; then we walked out on the front porch where Dad was smoking. I said, "Daddy, we are going to the meeting with the Nunley young folks." This time he didn't say, "No." I guess he saw our determination.

When we got to the brush arbor, it was full. Everything was different from the Baptist church. A young man and his sister began playing a guitar and singing beautifully. They sang songs like "I'm Going That Way," "O I Want to See Him," "The Glory-Land Way," and other songs. The preacher was a lady, Lillian White, a member of the Church of God, flag side. She preached with a heavy anointing about the Holy Ghost. I never went back to the Baptist church again.

I sought God in those Church of God meetings. They baptized me in the creek in Tracy City in the titles, Father, Son, and Holy Ghost. I was so happy! I sought the Holy Ghost but didn't receive it then.

I churned milk, caught four of our frying-sized chickens, molded a half-pound of butter and went to a whiskey-selling neighbor's house so I could go with a group of five in Mr. Patterson's homemade pick-up to the Cleveland, Tennessee, assembly meeting. I filled a shoe box with chicken and my daddy's Thermos jug full of coffee. I took a pillow and two quilts to sleep in a tent on the ground with straw for a bed. This time I had to beg Daddy a long time for permission to go.

"I don't have the money for you to go," he insisted. Daddy had plowed for Mr. Patterson, who owned the makeshift truck we were to ride in. Since spring Mr. Patterson had owed Daddy two dollars for the plowing.

"Mr. Patterson said I could ride with him for that two dollars he owes you," I begged.

"Well, looks like he won't pay me no how," Dad said.

"So okay, if you can get the money to get you something to eat." He didn't know my zeal! When I got through peddling my wares, I had two dollars. Hamburgers were only five cents, cakes were a nickel, but I also had a shoe box full of fried chicken and biscuits. When we ate our supper, I divided my food with all the others. I enjoyed being with those Holy Ghost people. I witnessed miracles of healing and people shouting at the assembly.

We moved to Taylorville, Illinois, where Dad drove a truck for my uncle and I entered high school. Our school band was to play in a concert on the town square. My parents agreed to attend the concert with me. We could hear the music two blocks away.

On our way, we passed an open-air Apostolic Church of Jesus Christ revival held in a former fruit market. "Of all things!" Mom commented as we stopped for the meeting. Dad stayed outside, but Mama and I sat up front. To my surprise, the Lord slayed Mama over the back of the seat. Was I embarrassed! The preacher and his wife, Silas and Maude Sanders, came off the sawmill plank platform to pray with Mama.

On the way home, I said, "Mama, I'm not going back anymore. He preached that there is not but one God. I believe there are three gods, and I know there are two."

"Lillian, he preached exactly what Brother Burrow preached," Mama answered.

Even though I had said, "I won't go back," the next night while Mama was getting ready to go, something got hold of me and I went with her. Again he preached about one God, but I kept going every night to the revival. Mama got baptized on Sunday.

In high school the Lord dealt with me very much. All

day in school I was miserable. I went to the preacher's house and said, "I want you to show me in the Bible about the one God." He handed me the Bible and told me what chapter and verse to read. I couldn't argue with the Word! The next Sunday I let him baptize me along with others. It was raining slightly, so I got sprinkled and baptized too! I didn't quite understand it, but a few days later, the general overseer from St. Louis came and gave us a three-week Bible study on Jesus' name and the Godhead. He gave all of us a paper with over a hundred verses of Scripture on the subject. I received the Holy Ghost in November 1936 after my water baptism in October.

A week or so later, the pastor asked me to teach the "card class" (small children) in Sunday school. We had only four classes: the card class, the junior class, and the intermediate class. The young people and the Bible class were together.

I sought God with all my heart. Soon the pastor appointed me as young people's secretary. The pastor's daughter, Stella, played the guitar in three keys: G, C, and D. She showed me how to play in the key of G. That Christmas I ordered a $9.95 guitar along with an instruction book from Speigel May Stearn catalog. I fasted and prayed and practiced on that guitar. Within six months I taught Stella the rest of the keys. But I never learned to play Mom's five-stringed banjo or fiddle.

We were in a revival on March 12, 1938, so Mama just thought I was going to service that Friday night when I wore my new blue dress. Our youth leader, Milford Leland Hedges, came by in his new dark blue suit. Helen Clemens, Merrill Hunt, and Beth Couples went with Milford and me to St. Louis, where we got married. About

4:30 A.M. I slipped in the house and got in bed with Mom, who asked, "What are you doing getting in this late?"

"Be quiet, don't wake Dad," I answered. Dad was asleep in the other room. I had to tell Mom so she would hush. When Dad found out, he started to tear up the marriage certificate and declared, "I'll have this annulled!" But Mom said, "No."

As I was just a sophomore, I planned to keep my marriage a secret. On Monday I went back to school as usual. When I came down from the second floor after cleaning the home-economics room, there was Mr. Walters, the principal. When he confronted me, I pleaded, "Please let me go on to school!"

"Lillian," he said, "we've never allowed this, but since it's you, I'm going to let you."

Oh, how I thanked him. I finished that year with five subjects. My junior year I carried a subject every period. At the end of the year, I needed only three and one-half credits to graduate. But the last month of the year, I became pregnant with our first child. Milford Leland, Jr., was born January 20, 1940. Later I got my high school diploma.

In school I was quite a basketball player. After I got the Holy Ghost, I quit playing ball. I had to "dress out," and the Lord told me that was wrong to dress in immodest apparel.

Milford and I worked in the Taylorville church a lot. Reverend C. W. Shew came to Springfield, Illinois, to begin a home missions church in a tent in the summer of 1946, and we helped him. He built a block basement. Brother J. H. Austin from Dyersburg, Tennessee, preached a revival and the work progressed.

In 1947 we took our truck and moved Brother Louie

and Sister Myrtle Jackson to Springfield to pastor the church that Brother Shew had started. We helped them until 1949 when we moved to Shelbyville, Illinois, to help Brother and Sister Claude Snodderly with a small, struggling church there. Our last child Edwina Rae was born.

Milford got a job driving a buggy 710 feet down in the coal mines in Pana, Illinois. Brother M. J. Wolff was our district superintendent. We attended camp meetings and youth camps at Murfreesboro, located on the highway. Our bathtub was a wash pan and our toilets were outdoor ones. There was no charge for our tent or our meals. The churches furnished the food, and we all did kitchen duty. In 1949 I drove our new two-ton truck loaded with supplies from the Pana church to the camp. Small tents served as dorms with piles of straw for beds. At the 1950 camp, Sister Gladys Robinson and I washed dishes all day. We talked, cried, and exchanged burdens. Her burden was Africa and mine was Tennessee.

We were happy working in Sister Eva Hunt's church in Pana. We sang in the choir, played the guitar, and worked in the altar. One night as I was praying for a young lady who was seeking the Holy Ghost, the Lord spoke to me and told me to go to Monteagle, Tennessee, and build a church. I didn't know that Brother B. H. Hite and his wife, Mary, had preached a revival there one summer thirty-five years before. Many were saved and healed in that great revival, but now they were scattered sheep.

We went to visit my mom's mother, who lived twelve miles from Monteagle. I had preached on Sunday night at the Emmanuel Church of Christ in Tracy City, pastored by Brother Henry Allison. As I drove through Monteagle, I began to weep uncontrollably.

Milford had a good job working five days a week plus much overtime, which was good money for those days! He was reluctant to quit and move to Tennessee. I just prayed and kept on serving the Lord.

Since I thought we wouldn't be able to go, I wrote to Sister Summer, a lady in the Emmanuel Church of Christ, "Get a group to hold prayer meetings in Monteagle."

One Friday in March 1951, I kept busy all day ironing and doing other household chores. I had supper cooking when Milford came in and said, "Get ready quick as you can. We're going to Tennessee!"

"We can't," I answered. "Next Friday is payday."

"Oh, I've borrowed the money. The Lord spoke to me in the mine today. We have to go."

We got in our 1949 Dodge, two-ton truck with our four children and headed for Tennessee. It rained most of the way. I had to hold seventeen-month-old Edwina on my lap all the way! We got into Monteagle the next Friday morning about 8 o'clock and drove through town looking the place over.

That night we went to Sister Summer's prayer meeting. Brother Allison asked me to preach. When I closed the service, I set chairs out and gave an altar call. Two ladies knelt and repented. Two years later one of those ladies, Earlene Milligan, married Milford's brother, Joseph B. Hedges. He pastored many years in Illinois.

Brother Allison asked Milford and me if we would go with him to Jasper, Tennessee, to hold a street meeting the next day. We readily agreed. While we were waiting in the car for Sister Summers to ride with us, Brother Allison said, "Sister Hedges, I feel you should take the work in Monteagle." Milford and I agreed upon that fleece to determine if we were truly in the Lord's will. We told Brother Allison that we thought it would be impossible. "We'll need a month or two to get ready to move."

We returned to Illinois and told our pastor, Sister Eva Hunt. "You have my blessing, but I do hate to see you go," she said. We loaded our clothes and furniture in our truck and 1941 Studebaker sedan and hitched the car to the truck.

We arrived in Monteagle the next afternoon, May 26, 1951. We had our first service June 3, 1951, with thirty-six people in attendance in D. and Deary King's house. Our services were Sunday morning Sunday school, Sunday night, Tuesday and Thursday nights, with young people's service on Saturday night.

We put tarp coverings over the cattle racks on our truck, put in benches, bedding, clothes, wash pans, and fourteen people, including our family, and went to the Tennessee District camp meeting at Perryville. Brother J. O. Moore, pastor at Henderson and district secretary, had built a cabin for his church. He let our ladies have a room with a pair of folding bedsprings. We made our bed on the floor with quilts over the springs. The men and boys slept in the truck, and Brother and Sister Wren Thomas made a pallet on the ground behind the cabin.

We knew only the J. H. Austins and the Norman Paslays, camp evangelists. Sister Hunt had written us a letter to give to the Tennessee District Board. We met the board and told them what we were doing in Monteagle. "Our attendance is about fifty," we said, so they gave us license. "The district has three home missions tents. You can have one to use this summer," they said.

We put the tent up on a vacant lot in front of where

the church is now. Brother and Sister Marvin Ellis preached a revival to a full tent for three weeks. We baptized several. We needed a lot to build a church on. Right in front of the tent was a fenced-in lot with a blackberry patch. As we looked at the lot, Mr. Brannan, the owner, asked, "Are you looking for me?"

Brother Ellis said, "We're looking for a lot to build a church on."

"I own this lot, and if you want it for a church, I'll almost give it to you. Can you pay $200?" Mr. Brannan asked.

"Yes," we answered as we had almost that much money saved since June third. This was the middle of August, and the revival was going strong! That Saturday night Brother Ellis took up enough money to finish the amount needed to close the deal on Monday. We also had over $35 a week to pay Brother Ellis. That was a pretty good offering for that day.

We bought the lot on Monday and rushed to Jasper to get the deed recorded. The lot was one hundred by one hundred and twenty-five feet. It was a hillside lot, so we dug out a basement and used the dirt to level the lot. We built a basement thirty-five by fifty feet. Back then banks considered church loans a bad risk, so we built as we got the money, holding services in the tent heated with an oil heater until November 22. That night snow caused the tent to fall! We rented a two-room house a block away for $10 until we finished the basement. We worshiped in the basement for ten years.

On April 4, 1962, we held our first service, a fellowship meeting, in the new auditorium. The Tennessee Ladies Auxiliary gave us a $500 offering, which helped us to get out of the basement.

Through those years many people repented, and we baptized them in the lakes and creeks. We've preached and helped to preach many funerals, married a few, and turned down a lot. We never performed a wedding ceremony for anyone with an ex-spouse. We had many revivals with preachers from all over the county. We took the young people every Saturday and held street meetings and jail services.

On March 3, 1956, we began a radio broadcast as we had another church going in South Pittsburg. We produced the radio program live unless I was out of town, when I tape-recorded the broadcast. We continued "The Pentecostal Hour" until January 16, 2000, when the station was sold, and the new owner raised our rates from $25 to $150. That priced all the preachers off the air. I spent forty-four years, nine months, and two weeks on radio. I really preached the one God, apostolic, Jesus Name baptism message all those years.

During those years I worked several jobs to do all the things I did. I sold insurance, ran a restaurant and taught school as a full-time substitute teacher.

On December 28, 1967, I faced the trial of my life! After twenty-nine years and nine months, my husband walked away from our marriage. We had a son and three daughters.

Through the years I had suffered the pain of my parents' separation and divorce. The other pain was the loss of my older brother, Ensign Chris Nelson Gibbs, a pilot in the U.S. Navy. He was missing in action in World War II in the third battle for the Leyte Gulf in the Philippines.

In 1972, I went full time for the church. God wonderfully blessed, and we added ten feet to the front of the church, rest rooms, nursery, and a foyer with a nice front. We have seen many people saved, evil spirits cast out, and healings. Sister Lossie Parrish died in the recovery room of the North Jackson, Alabama, hospital. Dr. Elmore had pronounced her dead. We went into the room, anointed her, and began praying, "Jesus, Jesus," with our hands on her forehead. She gasped and came back to life! Dr. Elmore came back into the room, stared at me, and continued to treat her. He told everyone, "No one can make me doubt the miracle power of God!" To God be the glory!

Our Sunday school attendance through much of those days was in the 70s and 80s, with a record Sunday of 113.

In March 1974 we went with a Tennessee group to the Holy Land. I borrowed a thousand dollars for my trip which cost a little over $700 including food, lodging, and transportation. A lady in the Monteagle church said, "I wouldn't think of borrowing money for anything like that!"

I told her, "This will last me a lifetime. You borrow money to buy a car which won't last long." We met with the tour in Atlanta, Georgia, flying from there to Shannon, Ireland. We flew from there to Nicosia, Cyprus, where we ate dinner and then traveled by bus to Famagusto, where we got on a Greek ship to Beirut, Lebanon. That ship docked at the pier and was our hotel as we toured Lebanon by bus. Brother W. M. Greer said to me, "Sister Hedges, we would never have dreamed that you and I would be on a bus in the Holy Land!"

We went from Lebanon to Damascus where Saul of Tarsus was smitten, to the street called Straight to Ananias's house. Later we sailed to Haifa, Israel. We had to go three miles out into the Mediterranean Sea to board the ship because explosives were going off near us and rocking the ship. We toured Israel by bus, guided by Moses Shuster. When Brother Nathaniel Urshan talked with him, he was concerned as we started into Jerusalem. He told us to get off the bus and walk six abreast since we were marching upward to Zion. He didn't know what he asked for! Brother L. H. Hardwick led the song and everyone sang. We stopped as we got across the city limits. Brother Enoch from Brother Hardwick's church began speaking in tongues, but no one interpreted. As we stood there in silent prayer, Moses ordered us to board the bus. He spoke in his language to the bus driver while looking at Brother Enoch, then he spoke to him. No response. He said to Brother Urshan, "That man speaks Hebrew."

Brother Urshan answered, "I'm sure he doesn't."

Then Moses insisted, "That man spoke in perfect Hebrew. He said, 'I am the God of this city. I will bring you through fiery times until you fall upon your knees and call upon My name. I am the Lord your God!'"

Don't doubt the miracle power of God! To God be the glory! We toured all of Israel.

In 1976 the United Pentecostal Church International had its first World Missions conference in Jerusalem. I borrowed $1000 and went with the UPC headquarters group. We had a great conference and toured Israel. With about eighty other people, I took a bus side trip to Greece and saw the places where Paul preached.

As we were going down the runway en route to London, suddenly the pilot aborted the flight. We sat on the tarmac for over three hours while workers repaired the plane. The stewardess came to me and asked, "Get your people to sing." I went to Helen Cole, Mike

Anderson, and Mildred Harper, who had been singing together on the tour. While they were singing, a woman named Stella had a son in the first-class cabin on his way to London for a brain tumor operation. She came running into our cabin asking for prayer. Brother Anderson took a handkerchief for all the preachers to lay hands on and pray. When they got to me, I anointed the handkerchief with my olive oil. We heard from Stella later that when the doctor X-rayed her son's head, the tumor was gone! That was the "airplane miracle!" We referred Stella to Brother Alan Demos, missionary in Athens, and she went to his services.

In 1980 we had another World Missions conference, and this time I went with Brother Donald Knight's group. We left Atlanta on Jordanian Airlines, out of New York to Amsterdam, then on to Amman, Jordan. We traveled from Jordan to Israel, toured Israel, then went back to Jordan. We went to Egypt and went up to the pyramid by the hotel. As we were flying back about to land in Amman, Jordan, the lights went out at the airport. "We'll have to go on to Damascus," the pilot said.

I prayed, "Lord, take care of us," and He did. We arrived back in Atlanta Thanksgiving Day 1980.

In 1977 my son-in-law was stationed in the U.S. Air Force at Bitburg, Germany. Wayne and Betty Schrum and family lived in Herforst, Germany, where he had a church in the ex-schoolhouse where they lived. They had services in the auditorium. I went to Frankfurt and visited them when Brother Hulon Myer was having a European conference, which we attended. Leaving the conference, we toured the country. Brother Schrum had a 1975 Chevy van. They took me to Luxembourg, France, Switzerland,

Liechtenstein, and Austria before returning to West Germany. We went on a boat out in Lake Chimsey to see the palace of King Leopold II, located on a small isle in the lake. As I looked at all that splendor, I thought, "Lillian Hedges, you are standing in a king's palace." The Lord said, "This is nothing compared to your palace in heaven." Tears rolled down my face.

We left there and drove to Dachau and the Holocaust prison for the Jews. I saw where Corrie ten Boom slept, the death chamber, the crematorium the pile of ashes with a granite stone on top saying, "To unknown millions." Sadness gripped me as I took a picture of that horror! My son-in-law, Wayne, said, "Mother, didn't you see that sign 'No Pictures'?"

"No," I answered, but the pictures were already shot. While I preached for Brother Schrum in Germany, Brother Robert Skimmyhorn from Goodlettsville filled in for me in Monteagle.

Through the years, I've had several close calls with death. In the late 50s, I knocked a chicken fryer full of steaming hot grease off my stove. The grease splashed on my left lower leg and fried my skin! I sat on the kitchen floor screaming and praying. God mightily touched my leg, and it was well in two or three days. However, later it would swell and be inflamed as it still does.

In May 1972 I had a blood clot in my lung that came from my leg, the doctor said.

On January 3, 1977, I went to Dr. Charles Couser in Cowan, Tennessee. He gave me a double shot of penicillin. I had taken it before, but this time it almost killed me. Dr. Couser and Dr. Horace Elkins, a dentist whose office was across the hall, worked with me one and a half hours before they revived me. When I came to, I vomited and then said, "I died and you've revived me!"

The doctor's wife said, "Oh, we know!"

I was vibrating really hard. I asked Dr. Couser, "Why am I shaking so?"

He said, "Your heart was stopped too long."

"How long?" I asked.

"Too long!" he answered.

The dentist has talked to me many times about this and he tells me, "It was terrible! You're a miracle to be alive and not a vegetable." This is documented. To God be the glory! I thank God every day for His healing power.

On February 22, 1977, my father's brother, Paul, was shot five times with a .38 pistol by his wife who was in a jealous rage. Dad called me to go to the Sewanee hospital. I went right into the emergency room. Paul said, "I'm dying and I'm not fit to die!" I anointed him, put my hand on his head and rebuked death in Jesus' name! Dr. Dudley Fort told me, "You saved his life. You can pray for any of my patients!" To God be the glory.

In 1978 I went back to visit my daughter, Betty, and her family in Germany. This time it was the military camp meeting in a round tent in the Plaza in Kaizerslaughtern, Germany. What a meeting we had! After the camp we toured Belgium and Holland. We stayed two nights with Brother and Sister Woosley, a licensed UPC minister holding services also at the army base at Hiest, Holland. He asked me to preach. That night several came to the altar. We went to Amsterdam and saw Corrie ten Boom's clock shop where she hid Jews during World War II. Later we toured Denmark and northern Germany. We stayed in a hotel on the Baltic Sea in Arousound, Denmark. I lay in bed that night and watched the ferry go across several times to Areo Island. In June there were only three hours of darkness. The next day we rode that ferry to Areo Island.

Denmark is the only country I've been in where I couldn't converse in English. Brother Wayne tried speaking in German, but they couldn't understand that either, so we pointed to what we wanted. We visited a cemetery with tombstones dated from 900 A.D. to 1500 A.D., which was very interesting.

In March 1981 Dad's wife died, so I took Dad to my house. He was blind and eighty-three years old. He died September 5, 1982. Brother L. H. Benson, Brother Franklin Hill, and Brother Darrell Pollock preached his funeral. The Pollocks sang.

In 1983 the U.S. Air Force stationed Wayne Schrum in Weathersfield, England. In June I visited them and we toured England, Scotland, and Wales. The British Isles camp meeting was in session at Swanick, England. Brother Robert McFarland was the regional field supervisor for Europe and the Middle East. What a great visit!

In 1984 we felt it was time for a church in South Pittsburg, Tennessee, as God had dealt with me since 1953. No Jesus Name church of any kind had ever been there, but my radio program, The Pentecostal Hour, was heard there. We talked to Brother Sam Chessor about it, and he agreed. So Brother and Sister Walter Boudin and I spent two weeks trying to find a building. We told Brother Chessor that we would help him. We went to Mr. Howard Horn, who owned the old theater, to ask if we could rent it. A Church of Christ pastor had been renting it. The Mormons, the Seventh Day Adventists, a bowling alley, and a package beer place had all tried to rent it. Mr. Horn said, "I don't know what my church will say, but I'm going to let you all have it."

Brother Chessor then declined to come. I cried. My heart was broken. As I was praying, God told me, "You go!" I brought it before the Monteagle church. To my surprise, they were excited about it. Brother Benson and Brother Gerald Davis, home missions director, gave us $500 to pay the utilities and the first month's rent. For nine days ten saints from Monteagle helped me to clean it up and get it ready for service. We began with a ten-day revival. God blessed! The next summer Brother Benson had the Tennessee Youth Corp under Brother Marty Johnson to come and work the town. Brother Davis preached the night services.

In January 1985 we left for the World Missions conference in Manila, Philippines. We had a great conference, and then we went to Hong Kong for two days. Then five train carloads left Hong Kong for Canton, China.

That year we bought a house at 907 Cedar Avenue in South Pittsburg. Money came in from so many. We repaired the house, using it for church services for over three years while working on the church building on the lot next door, now used as our parking lot. We received $5,000 from Sheaves for Christ! We built a basement and had services there while finishing the sanctuary.

Many people helped us build. We had a contractor do the basement and rough in the plumbing. Brother Lewis Summers and his work buddy from the Monteagle church did the electrical work. Others donated labor, including my brother, Edwin, from Taylorville, who spent his vacation working. The bank loaned us money for the materials. Now the bank is paid, the church is out of debt, and it is insured for $240,000.

From 1949 to 2001, I have missed only nine General Conferences. I missed the one in Philadelphia. I couldn't go there and to the Holy Land, so I chose the Holy Land. Since attending my first camp meeting in 1951, I have missed only the one when I was with my daughter in Swanick, England. I was at the first youth camp on Holiness Hill and always enjoy working in the youth camps. The work of God means everything to me. This is my life!

But my life has not always been a bed of roses. I've had some serious health problems. In May 1979 I had gall bladder surgery and was hospitalized twelve days. Pneumonia has attacked me several times. On May 24, 1998, I had a severe heart attack. I was at the South Pittsburg church and in great pain. While I was praying, the white church walls turned black. I knew I was dying, so I cried, "Death, I rebuke you in Jesus' name." Then the black walls turned white again. I kept on praying and then played the piano, led the singing, and taught the adult Sunday school class, followed by a short devotion, and dismissed. As I was getting in my car, I told Sister Geneva Dismukes, "I'm going home and going to the emergency room."

"You are not," she answered. "Shut that door and get in my car. I'm taking you to the hospital."

When we got to the hospital, only five blocks away, the doctor said, "You are going to the intensive care unit. You've had a heart attack." Wednesday he sent me by ambulance to Park Ridge Hospital in Chattanooga. On Friday, I had open heart surgery with four bypasses.

Arthritis plagues my knees and other joints. On

September 5, 2001, I had three light heart attacks, was treated in Sewanee Hospital, and then sent on to Park Ridge Hospital for two arteriograms. My main artery was blocked. They ran an instrument through a vein into the back side of my heart, which was getting no blood. I had to sign a paper acknowledging that the procedure could kill me. The doctor told me that I was dying. Again I rebuked death in Jesus' name, and the doctor looked strange. But I am still living! As of April 17, 2002, I am still pastoring the South Pittsburg UPC church.

In January 2001 I went to the Philippine Crusade. Thirty-five to forty crusade teams ministered throughout the island. I went with the Manila group. Brother T. F. Tenney was one of the leaders. The meetings were awesome! I stayed in the Manila Hotel, and Sister Mallory invited me to go up to their suite where General MacArthur's headquarters had been. Some of his possessions were still there. We held the meeting across the street in front of the hotel at the open-air arena. They estimated the crowd at a hundred thousand! Throughout one island thousands received the Holy Ghost.

God has blessed me with my own home, a two-family house located one block from the Monteagle church. My daughter Edwina and family live in the other apartment. We have made several improvements since purchasing the house.

For a year and a half, my daughter Betty and son-in-law Wayne Schrum served as my associate pastors in both the Monteagle and South Pittsburg churches until I turned the Monteagle church over to Brother Schrum on November 6, 1992.

In 1995 the World Missions conference was held in

Athens, Greece. This time I went with the UPCI head-quarters group, and again we had a side tour to Israel. We planned to fly out of Nashville to Charlotte, North Carolina, on to New York, then to Athens. On Sunday night a week before we were to leave, I went into the hospital at Sewanee with severe bronchitis and extremely low potassium. I was seriously sick. I told the doctor on Wednesday morning that I had my ticket to Greece and Israel and was to leave at 10:40 Monday morning. I expected him to say, "You can't go." But he threw up his hands and said, "You can go with all your prayers and what I'm going to do for you!"

We left, like he said, although I did ask for wheelchair assistance at all the airports. I was very weak but I made it! I had special prayer the first night of the conference. Sister Judy Bentley, Brother C. M. Becton, and other ministers laid hands on me and really prayed. We had a great conference, toured the country, and flew to Israel. Our guide in Israel was named Rickey. "That means Rebecca in our language," she explained. I witnessed constantly to her, and she was very receptive. Often she had me read the Bible at the appropriate times on the tour. When we arrived at the river Jordan, a lady from Florida wanted to be baptized. As we left, Rickey named the next destination, but everyone in the back of the bus said, "No, we've got to go back to the river to baptize this lady."

Brother Norris and Brother Hodges said, "No, she has to be counseled."

I called out, "No, she only has to repent!"

Pastor Gordon from Denver said, "That's right. Get over there, Sister Hedges, you're the most capable on this bus."

I got my Bible out of my purse and quickly read as I showed her the verses of Scripture on baptism. We prayed with her for repentance. For a few minutes I wondered if I would have to baptize her as sick as I was, but a brother said that he would go in with Brother Gordon, who was partially blind. When we arrived at the place for the baptism, Brother Coots from Texas was baptizing others, so he baptized this lady also. We went back to the bus where Rickey had observed all this. We prayed for the lady who had been baptized, and soon she was speaking in tongues beautifully. All it takes is to repent and be baptized in Jesus' name!

On June 3, 1997, my mother died at the age of ninety-seven. Brother L. H. Benson and Brother Wayne Schrum preached her funeral. I was blessed to have my parents live to a ripe old age and be saved.

On June 3, 2001, the Monteagle church celebrated fifty years since the first service. Brother George Cohron, the pastor, planned a wonderful celebration. The crowd packed the building. Since I had started the church and still pastored South Pittsburg, they honored me that day. Brother Harold Jaco, Tennessee district secretary, and Brother Philip Swinford were the main speakers. The Tullahoma church choir, the Cohron trio, Edwina, and I sang. After the service that afternoon, Betty Ladd catered a special dinner and served it outside under a tent. They also honored me with a most generous offering, for which I was very grateful!

I have gone to the "Because of the Times" meetings in Alexandria, Louisiana, for many years. I enjoy them very much. I love all the meetings—camp meetings, youth camps, conferences, fellowship meetings, revivals, and regular services. I've been blessed to get to go to all those meetings! It's been such a pleasure meeting and knowing so many of God's wonderful people. Imagine what it will be like in the New Jerusalem!

by Lillian Hedges

Lillian Gibbs Hedges and brothers
Edwin and Nelson

Lillian Gladys Gibbs Hedges

Five generations, seated left to right: Parlee Numley, Leland Hedges, and Florence Adam; standing, Lillian Hedges and Minnie Gibbs

Monteagle church in 1963

Lillian Hedges

Lillian Gladys Gibbs Hedges

Left to right back row: Leland, Lillian, and Milford.
Front row: Sharon, Betty, and Edwina, 1951

CHAPTER Nine

Lela Chumney Holland

Sometimes my grandchildren will say, "Gannie, tell us about the 'olden times.'" This request is a grim reminder that I'm living in a generation that's far different from the one in which I was born. Let me tell you a few things that I know will seem unreal to you in the fast pace in which we now live.

In the year 1913 Lela Mae Chumney was born into a home that certainly lacked many of the comforts of this life, but it was a peaceful home. My parents were old-fashioned shouting Methodist people. We five children were taught respect for God and for each other. I do not remember any of us ever sassing our parents, and to call someone a liar was certainly a "no, no" at our house.

I remember vividly a rambling old farmhouse, a roaring fire in the fireplace, and my mother carding sheep's wool into batts. She then spun those batts (slender rolls of wool about twelve inches in length) into thread on the spinning wheel. Those wool stockings that Mother knit on her hand-powered knitting machine were warm, but, oh, how they did scratch!

As I grew older, I was privileged to attend a one-room country school where the only heat was a wood stove. The water fountain was a bucket filled with water and brought up from the spring under the hill. I can still hear the children saying, "Teacher, may I pass the water?" This consisted of the bucket being passed around the room and everyone drinking from the same dipper unless by chance you possessed a five-cent folding drinking cup. Unhealthy? Sure! But at least we didn't have any of the diseases that the world is plagued with today.

What a peaceful world! There was no need for locks on the doors in those days. Neighbors helped their fellowman, and when someone's cow was dry, the neighbors shared their milk and butter. If sickness or bad times came to someone, the burden was shared by all. This was the kind of atmosphere in which I grew up.

I do not remember when I first began to pray, but I do remember one of my first childhood prayers. It was this: "Star light, star bright, first star I've seen tonight; I wish I may, I wish I might, have the wish I wish tonight!" Then according to the fable you were to make a wish, step five steps backward, reach behind you, and find that for which you had wished. I remember repeatedly asking to find a nickel. To me I was looking beyond the star and to a God who was up there somewhere. A nickel meant a lot to children in those days.

As I grew older and attended the summer protracted revivals, I would see older ladies shout, and a hunger came into my heart that someday maybe I would feel like they felt. When I had just became a teenager, I felt a strong conviction from God in an old-time Methodist church. I went to an altar and did as I was instructed to do. I was baptized and adhered to the teaching of the church, but there was still an emptiness that I longed to have filled.

This was before the days of transportation to school, so there were very few in those days who attended high school. I had finished the eighth grade at the country school, which was a six-mile walk each day. I took an extra year at this school. Then a way was opened for me to attend high school. I had to stay away from home. It was not easy, but I had a deep desire to get an education and progress academically. I loved sports, especially basketball. I would forego my lunch anytime to get to play in the old ramshackle gymnasium.

I did not have school supplies to spare as children have today. My school tablet was a five-cent rough-leafed tablet. At midterm and final test, I was privileged to have a ten-cent slick-leafed tablet. I was not alone in this situation, nor was I a pauper. There was just very little affluence in those days.

I roomed with two girls one year while in high school. We carried our groceries from home, and our conveyance was a wagon. We went to our room for lunch. I remember one of our regular noon meals. It was thickened gravy, jelly, and biscuits left over from breakfast. In 1930, when I was a sophomore, I stayed at the principal's home and helped his wife with the housework for my room and board.

During this summer a great revival was in progress at the Scotts Hill Holiness Church. The school board had passed a ruling that students could not be out at night after 10 P.M. However, because of the great move of the Spirit in this revival, God surpassed the ruling!

One day there had been a baptizing near where I was staying. I decided to go to church. A girl who went to this church regularly sat with me that night. Brother Pitts Graves and family were holding the revival. When the invitation was given, this girl said, "Lela, let's go to the altar."

So many things came into my mind such as, "You belong to the church, what will people think, etc." This was my reasoning: *I'll go with her even though I don't need to go because staying at the bench might keep her from doing what she should do.* I'm sure I looked like I needed to go. My hair was cut short, my face and lips were painted, and I wore a sleeveless dress. Although I had gone to pray for this girl, I had not been at the altar long until I realized that I was the one standing in the need of prayer. Oh, how those people could pray, and they were all praying at the same time! I tried to pray, but I soon realized that I needed to go a different route. I began to repent.

Brother L. J. Thompson's wife began to pray and to instruct me. She said, "Maybe it's your short hair."

I said, "It will never be cut again." I meant it then, and I still mean it now after seventy years. I would not even allow chewing gum to be cut out of my hair.

Sister Thompson also said, "Maybe you should not wear sleeveless dresses."

I replied, "I'll never wear another one." To keep that declaration, I had one short green jacket that I wore with every sleeveless dress I possessed. By the time the summer season was over, that jacket was threadbare in the back and pulled at the armholes.

A minister told me in later years what his thoughts were when he saw me going to the altar. *Poor little thing; she will never hold out with her church background and also her love for sports and worldly pleasures.* But he did not know my hunger for the things of God.

In August 1930, I was baptized in Jesus' name in the same old millpond in which I had previously been baptized. The experience of the Holy Ghost baptism was all very new to me, and this message was not very popular in those days. I received good blessings and thought perhaps I had the Holy Ghost, but there was still an uncertainty. I did not want to disclaim this experience, but I still hungered for greater evidence.

In October 1930, a few of the young girls from the church were in a grove meeting. I still remember my prayer: "Lord, if anyone here does not have the Holy Ghost, would you please fill them now?" A mighty rushing wave of glory enveloped me, and utterances that I had never heard came forth from my mouth! It seemed that the birds in the trees had joined in the chorus of my praises to God! I even opened my eyes to see if this were true. Oh, how I thank God for the validity of this wonderful truth and experience. I had found that for which my heart had hungered!

My high school ambitions changed. I was supposed to be on the first team basketball at the opening of the season. I'll never forget the day I turned in my basketball suit and told the coach that my heart was no longer in the game. May I say for the youth of today that God still expects the same in your consecration. This was my sophomore year.

The economy was very bad, and it seemed at times that I would not be able to finish high school. When I was a senior, my shoes became so worn that I had to wear my galoshes to keep my shoes on my feet. Still I trudged along, studied from borrowed books, but the dear Lord was teaching me lessons in perseverance. I witnessed in school. We would bring our songbooks and sing at the noon hour. Many, many young people found the Lord.

It was during this time that the girls from the Scotts Hill Holiness Church began having grove meetings behind Brother and Sister L. J. Thompson's home every Sunday afternoon. We had great times! It was becoming my lot to direct these prayer meetings. Little did I know what God was preparing me for.

I remember especially one Sunday afternoon we met for the grove service. The power of God began to fall; and when we finally became "earth-bound" again, six people had received the Holy Ghost, and a full moon was shining brightly. We made our way to the church, which was nearby, and went in shouting over the trophies God had given us. What a stir God allowed to come upon the church in those days! Can it be repeated? Yes! If God's people meet God's conditions!

In the spring of 1933, I finished high school. The Lord had given me a good mind and motivation to study. I was honored to be valedictorian of the 1933 class at Scotts Hill High School.

It was the custom for the different churches in town to take turns inviting the speaker for the commencement or baccalaureate service. This was the year for the Holiness church to invite the speaker. Brother A. D. Gurley was chosen. I shall never forget that message. His text was

Matthew 6:33: "But seek ye first the kingdom of God, and his righteousness; and all these things shall be added unto you." What a message anointed and delivered in true Brother Gurley style. What a day!

When he was finished, someone said, "If he can sing like he preaches, we must hear him." They found an old guitar, and one of the school board members gave permission for him to use it. I remember so well the song he sang: "Goodbye World of Sin and Sadness." The chorus went like this:

> "Goodbye world of sin and sadness
> Goodbye sorrow, woeful pain,
> For I've met the man of gladness
> Jesus, Jesus is His name.
>
> You have lost your fond attraction,
> In my heart no more they lie.
> I've become the Lord's relation;
> I will say to you goodbye."

Some of the businesspeople of this town wanted to help me go to college and prepare to be a teacher. It was enticing, but God had other things in mind for a poor, struggling young girl. My family could not understand my longing for the service of God.

After school was out, I was no longer near enough to attend church very often. I had such a vehement desire to live for God that I was driven more and more to prayer. I had a place in the woods a little way from the house that I resorted to three times a day to pray. I remember once when I was sick that I felt I had to get to my place of prayer. I walked down there, but I was in such intense pain that I crawled part of the way back. I was still in God's training program. I must learn to "endure hardness, as a good soldier of Jesus Christ." I did not understand what was really happening in my life. I wanted to work with souls, but it was far from my expectations that I could ever be worthy or qualified to be a minister.

One day at the church, God confirmed my calling. On this Sunday when service was dismissed, there was a real burden to stay and pray; several stayed. During the afternoon, prayer was constantly in progress. People passing the church came in to investigate. Many of them got under conviction, came to the altar, and received the Holy Ghost. Later in the afternoon God began to speak to me about the work He wanted me to do. I questioned, "Lord, I'm so ill-equipped. My family will not understand because they're not Pentecostal. I don't even own a Bible." All that I had was a little paperback New Testament. Incidentally, I would put this little testament under my straw hat so that I could read when I sat down to rest while working in the fields. God appeared to me, not visibly, but speaking to me. I became very weak and fell back in a faint. I had been permitted to lay hands on people that day, and they had received the Holy Ghost. I was made to understand that God was equipping me with what was needed to bring people to God. He would send the conviction, sinners would submit to it, and He would allow me to be used in this manner of laying on of hands—a promise from God!

This is how the Lord has blessed my ministry for many years. I have been very shy about pushing myself in this matter. Rather I've chosen to stay in the background, being a lady minister. I've seen many filled with the Holy

Ghost through the years. This happened when I was able to remember what the Lord had confirmed that my ministry would be. I do not believe in gadgets or gimmicks in this ministry.

During 1933 Brother E. J. Douglas preached a brush arbor revival at a little community named Shady Hill. I was asked to come and sing and work in the altar. I still was unaware of what God had in mind for my life.

One night it rained, and the evangelist could not get there. He advised me to take the service. Scared? I guess so! The only Bible I had was the small New Testament that had been presented to me on Class Day when I finished high school. Brother Douglas had been building up to the place to give an altar call but had not yet given one. The subject of my first sermon was, "And thou shalt call his name JESUS: for he shall save his people from their sins" (Matthew 1:21). I don't know how God did it, but He did! I brought the message and gave the altar call. There were six in the altar including a man living nearby who had already gone to bed. He heard the service, God spoke to him, he arose, dressed, and came to the altar. There were six conversions that night. Oh, for the same obedient hungry hearts that are willing to be touched by the gentle hand of God!

It was back to this brush arbor that I was invited to come and preach in the fall of 1933. This was my first preaching appointment. Thank you, Sister Lois Milam, a dear Pentecostal lady, for going along with me. You'd be surprised at our way of conveyance. A nice man of a Pentecostal family offered us a ride on a wagon loaded with cottonseed. It was not a Cadillac, but it surely beat walking about ten miles.

I still didn't have a Bible when I accepted the invitation to go there and preach. A dear, distant cousin, Florence Essary, gave me enough money to order a Bible from Sears, Roebuck and Company. The cost was $2.19, and, oh, how thankful I was for this precious Book! It didn't have a concordance, and it was rather amusing to see me trying to find a verse of Scripture I wanted to use, maybe after church service had begun. On this, my first appointment, my Scripture text was "Examine yourselves, whether ye be in the faith" (II Corinthians 13:5). My topic was "Taking Tests."

From there I began to get calls for revivals. When I packed an old, metal suitcase with what few clothes I had, my songbook and Bible, my parents could not understand my calling. I can understand their fears for my safety, but I can truthfully say that by the Lord's help and choosing well with whom I worked, there were no "shady" situations. Sister Ola (Clenny) Stanfill and I worked together some in those early days, and we enjoy reminiscing when we are together.

I think the first converts to be baptized in a revival I conducted were in Brother Guy Webb's church at Morris Chapel, Tennessee, in January 1934. It was cold! Since there were no baptisteries in those days, a big log fire was built on the bank of the creek. Brother Webb was a small man, and some of the converts were getting a blessing and in no hurry to exit that icy water. Evidently Brother Webb did not share their desire for remaining in the creek. He said, "I thought I'd freeze to death." Brother Webb did a great work for the rural churches of West Tennessee.

In another of the churches that Brother Webb pastored, I was conducting a revival that same year at Adamsville, Tennessee. On Easter Sunday a large crowd was expected. A baptismal service was scheduled before church on Sunday morning in Brother Jack Scott's stock pond. I was staying in the Scott's home during the revival. I shall never forget starting through a large hall in the house and meeting some young people from Beauty Hill Pentecostal Church near Bethel Springs, Tennessee. I did not know that one of those young men would play a vital part in my future.

Thank you, Brother Carlos Holland, the young man I met that day, for being such a nice, considerate friend in the months that followed. Our friendship was certainly never accompanied with petting or familiarity. In fact, there was never a kiss or holding of hands until we were man and wife. We wrote letters about once a week. He visited my revivals when they were near enough. Brother Holland was from a large Pentecostal family of nine boys.

On December 1, 1934, we were married by a justice of the peace. Church weddings were almost unheard of in those days, especially for people who were short on funds as we were; but our union has outlasted many weddings with all the "trimmings." We are in our sixty-eighth year.

We spent our first winter at his parents' home. At times there were as many as fifteen at Pappaw Holland's to be fed. Flour was bought by the barrel, and corn was taken to the grist mill be to ground. It fell my lot to make the biscuits for breakfast—125 biscuits. It was pretty good "sopping" with McNairy County rabbits and thickened gravy. I'm sure the rabbit population was greatly diminished that winter. This was quite an experience for me as I had been reared in a much smaller family.

It was not easy going for us that first winter. My husband's first job was checking lumber at a sawmill for seventy-five cents a day. Our first automobile was a 1917 T-model "stripdown," nothing but the running gear. In fact, a tomato crate was used for a seat to drive it home. The cost was $7.50. Carlos and his brother, Cleo, were partners in buying the vehicle. They paid $5 down and the remainder on time. When we could afford it, we paid the remainder and bought Cleo's investment. Now it was all ours!

I preached a revival at Adamsville, Tennessee, in the spring, and we bought a green sedan car body, which was put on this vehicle. Now we could be dry when it rained. Although we were poor, we were blessed of God!

I had held a ministerial license for possibly a year with the Pentecostal Church, Incorporated. Brother T. C. Montgomery, overseer of the Church of the Lord Jesus Christ, ministered in the area in which we now lived. I was ordained in the ministry in this organization in 1935. Later, though, it was my desire to be ordained by the ministers and organization that I knew in the beginning. In 1938 in Scotts Hill Holiness Church during a district conference, I was ordained by the ministers of the Pentecostal Church, Incorporated. Later they united with the Pentecostal Assemblies of Jesus Christ to become the United Pentecostal Church International.

In September of the following year, 1935, our baby girl came to bless our home. In those days, and especially in that community, people believed in trusting God for healing. We had only a midwife attendant at Carlene's birth.

In February 1936 we were called to Cleveland, Tennessee, to help in church work there. We had some interesting experiences while in that eastern part of the state. In one instance, we went on a preaching appointment to Copperhill, Tennessee. This is the area where all the timber and vegetation had been killed by the sulphuric acid fumes emanating from the Copperhill plant. I ministered that day standing on the porch of a family who lived in that area. That in itself was not unusual, but the family animals were roaming around loose. Maybe I lost my unction, not knowing at what time I could get "butted" from my position by one of the goat critters marching through the hall of the house. We stayed six months at Cleveland before returning home to McNairy County.

We moved into a little one-room log house near the Holland family home. This was not a classy residence, but it was home to us. Snakes and rats inhabited the house with us, but thanks to the Lord, we were never bitten.

Our oldest son Paul was born in March 1937. We had our cow, hogs, and chickens. We pastored some little country churches and were usually paid in canned goods and feed for the animals. During summer revival season, my husband had to work, so he would come on weekends.

We were away so much that the chickens decided that they were "wild fowls." Between revivals, when we were home, the only way we could have a fryer to eat was to go "chicken hunting" and shoot one with the gun.

Mack, our youngest son, arrived in July 1939. When he was born, his head was opened too much; and as we were still depending upon God for our help, we did not seek a physician's aid. One night I knew we desperately needed God's help in this, so I laid my hands on his little head and asked God to heal our baby. Thank God, He did just that! The enlarged opening began closing and became normal. I really don't see how people exist without a friend like this lovely Lord.

When Mack was about two months old, I took him and went to Mason Wells, near Jackson, Tennessee, for a revival. My ever-faithful husband kept the two older children at the home of some very dear friends. Thank you, John Nealus and Alice Nold for being such a help to us in those days. I would take the infant baby outside before church began, feed him, and pray that he would sleep while I preached. He slept on a pillow on the front pew. Someone watched him for me.

In those days so many people came to our altars seeking God that there was hardly room. In this particular revival, many people were seeking and finding the Lord. A young lady from a Presbyterian family was being greatly blessed of God. I saw her mother come rushing down the aisle of the church. I began to pray; and before she reached the altar, she fell prostrate in the floor. I immediately went to her. When I knelt beside her, she was speaking in a beautiful heavenly language. I hope when we get over yonder, we can renew acquaintance with some of these people.

A parcel of land was purchased for camp meeting near beautiful Pickwick Lake not far from Iuka, Mississippi. Tennessee, Alabama, and Mississippi comprised the Southeastern District. Brother A. D. Gurley was district superintendent. The first camp meeting was held in 1941. Produce was donated and a beef was fattened. A pea patch was planted on the grounds. Chickens were brought live and put in pens. Volunteers picked and shelled the peas for cooking. Another group killed and picked the chickens, and others split the stove wood.

To have a change in the menu, we offered to bring the meat for one day. We cleared it with Brother Gurley to bring some young goats. No, we didn't take them live. We lived within driving distance of the camp meeting. The meat was prepared, packed in ice, and we left for Pickwick with the meat for that day.

Brother and Sister Gurley met us at the kitchen. Sister Gurley said, "We're naming this goat 'Old Mutton.'" It was cooked as only Brother George White could cook.

I heard different remarks that day about the meat, such as, "This is the best meat we've had." Then someone else remarked, "But I think it was goat instead of mutton." Great days! Wonderful memories!

One day I had gone to the service before I went to the kitchen to work. When I got to the kitchen, I began to tell those there about the service. A young girl humbly spoke up, "I wish I knew the Lord." I told her that she could find Him right then. The big dinner pots were pushed to the back of the old army field range stove. Down on our knees in the sawdust we went in prayer, and she found the Lord! The young girl was Hermie Plunk, who is now the wife of Brother W. D. McCollum.

The tabernacle was a tent and the pews were planks laid on concrete blocks with no backs. The dormitories were, for the most part, cots under trees and tents. There was one small facility for women built above the kitchen, which was quite warm!

Sleeping accommodations were very difficult to find. One night after the service was dismissed and people had returned to their sleeping places, some elderly men decided to stay in the big tent. They pushed some planks or benches together and arranged a place to sleep.

They lay down for a night's repose. Soon they were aroused by some people entering the tent. It wasn't very long until a prayer meeting was in progress. After a time of praying, the group began to sing "Silent Night, Holy Night." This was quite an appropriate melody for the sleepers!

The ministry was superb. Brother Frank J. Ewart taught on "Jesus, the Man and the Mystery." A quartet from Laurel, Mississippi, sang "I Possess a Lot in Canaan." Brother Vol Sumrall, I can still hear and see you in my memory as you sang.

At the foot of the hill lay beautiful Pickwick Lake. Converts were baptized there in Jesus' name in the afternoon. Also at a certain time of day the men and boys went to a secluded cove where they took their daily baths. The accommodations may have been primitive, but this was camp meeting, camp meeting style!

Little did we know what God had in His plan for us. In 1939 we accepted the pastorate of the little church at Sweetwater near Hohenwald, Tennessee. We came once a month for revivals for about two years. Brother A. D. Gurley and Brother J. C. Brickey had ministered in this area in the 1920s. The work had been left and had been "ill-used" in the years that followed. It had been a long time since there had been a Holy Ghost outpouring in Lewis County. Few were filled with the Holy Ghost. It was certainly a ripe field when God allowed us to come.

In October 1941 we loaded all of our goods and "chattels," including our two cows and the hay, on Tab Hill's truck and headed for Lewis County. Sister Kate Deavers had provided us, rent free, with a little four-room house. God had already begun to fill people with the Holy Ghost even before we moved.

That fall and winter of 1941-42 tried our faith for food and provisions. There were no jobs. That meant no tithes from the church to speak of. That winter was a trying time for my husband. He had always provided for the family. I remember two jobs he had that winter. He and a man in the church dug a well in snowy weather for a few dollars each. The other job consisted of he and the same man skinning a mule that had died and selling the hide for $10. Bless you, my dear husband, for standing by us in our work for God.

But there's another side to this story. While all this was transpiring, a revival like this area had not known for many years was in progress. We had an old model car and an open two-wheeled trailer. There was no church in Hohenwald, so we loaded all the people we could get in the car and on the trailer and went to the little Sweetwater church. In cold, snowy weather, we carried as many as nineteen to church. True, when we came to a hill, the trailer riders got off and walked up the hill. What wonderful, wonderful times! A baby child who was paralyzed from its waist down was miraculously healed! There were many other great moves of God. We carried a busload to Corinth, Mississippi, in February 1942 for Brother A. D. Gurley to baptize. Twenty-seven were baptized. We felt definitely that God had called us to build a church in Hohenwald. Pledges were taken, and some of the dear people sold items of furniture to pay their pledges.

We began looking for a lot in town. We were told that no one would sell us a lot on which to build a Pentecostal church. God, who is above all in power and might, provided us with a beautiful lot and the means to pay for it. Brother A. D. Gurley, who was district superintendent at that time, secured us a loan for $3,000 from a lady he knew in Bemis, Tennessee.

In March 1942 Brother L. J. Thompson and Brother Walter Herndon of West Tennessee came and showed Brother Holland how to lay blocks for the First Pentecostal Church in Hohenwald. Brother Holland began laying the blocks on the church and would only take from the building fund the sum of $1 per day. There was some volunteer labor, but he and a young man in the church by the name of Ralph Sims principally erected the church in Hohenwald.

Brother A. D. Gurley came for a tent revival in August 1942. Converts were taken to the beautiful stream of this area almost daily to be baptized. The church grew soundly and rapidly.

Those were trying times with no jobs to be had. Brother Holland had taken a job as a mechanic for $17.50 per week. When we got the church to the place we could have service in it, Brother Holland went to Detroit, Michigan, to work. That I could not bear! He stayed three weeks. I wrote for him to please come home; we would make it somehow. He returned home on a Monday morning. He had tried many times to get a job at the local General Shoe (now GENESCO) plant, but to no avail. He went the next morning and was told to come in for an interview the next day. Needless to say, we prayed. The future of the church in Hohenwald and our future was at stake. He was hired, and in less than a year entered supervisory training. He worked in that capacity for thirty-one years. Thank God, He never forgets us!

In September 1943 another baby girl, Marilyn, came into our home. She, along with our other three children, have blessed our home.

The church was growing to such an extent that we felt it necessary to build a Sunday school annex. Ours was the first church in town to build such an addition. By this time we were averaging over one hundred. We had many great revivals. Only eternity will reveal what was actually accomplished.

We had some great evangelists in the 1940s including the Rexie Wilcox and Cleveland Becton team. Brother Becton had just begun to present lessons on the flannel-graph board. We really enjoyed having those young men in our home, and what a wonderful revival we had! Then we were blessed with a young evangelist by the name of O. W. Williams. Hohenwald was his first revival. He later served as district superintendent of Texas.

We were taking the young workers and musicians to schoolhouses and nearby towns, and it seemed God was ready for an even greater harvest of souls. We were averaging around 130 in Sunday school. The church was free of debt and owned a parsonage. In early 1950 we left the church. My top salary was thirty-five dollars per week.

We worked in Waynesboro, Tennessee, and really God had spoken to us about building a church there. A lady offered us land, but other plans were made and we did not get to fulfill our desires.

We worked in Linden, Tennessee, for two years in the early 1950s. We were able to buy a parcel of land for a church. We kept this land, and in the 1970s a church was built on it.

I was elected the first Ladies' Auxiliary president of Tennessee in 1952. It was my privilege to travel to the various churches and organize ladies' groups and also the sectional groups. It was a small beginning, and we had no funds to speak of. I'm glad to have had a small part in this great work. After three years, I asked to be relieved as we were engaged in building a church in Lexington, Tennessee.

Brother W. M. Greer, the Tennessee district superintendent, asked us to start a work in the city of Lexington, Tennessee, in 1952. In August 1952, Brother E. E. McNatt held a tent meeting on the lot where the Pentecostal church in Lexington now stands. We had some wonderful help while we worked in Lexington. The C. B. Creasy family and others were great helpers. After this revival, we secured the American Legion building for services. We had nineteen in Sunday school the first Sunday. In the fall of this same year, a basement church was built on two beautiful lots on Natchez Trace Drive. The first service was conducted in the basement of the church on the first Sunday of December 1952.

God really blessed the efforts there. The initial building was paid for. Also a three-room apartment was built on the back of the church and was free of debt. We drove from Hohenwald, a distance of fifty-five miles one way, and worked there for five years.

When we had around seventy-five in Sunday school, we felt that the church could support a pastor. The dear people there asked us to select whom we wanted to come. Brother W. D. McCollum was elected as pastor. We left after five good years. This was the last church we built as a family. Our children were grown and preparing for their individual lives.

In 1959 I had a very serious surgery in which two-thirds of my stomach was removed. During the 1960s I completely lost my voice as far as being able to preach or sing. I could not sit idle, so I began working with the Lewis County school system as a substitute teacher. In 1965 I was asked by the superintendent of schools to help organize and teach kindergarten. I returned to school in the summers and taught during the school term. I enjoyed seventeen years working in the school system.

During the years I taught, I always had a time of devotion and singing each day. On one occasion, the children were very noisy; and because I had a broken arm, it was hard to maintain order. I called them to order and said, "I'm going to pray for you children to be quiet." They were astonished, but it worked!

Brother Holland retired from the local GENESCO plant and spent his last eight work years with the Lewis County school system as maintenance and transportation supervisor. We are both retired now. He works in his woodcraft shop and sells all he cares to make to the Wal-Mart stores.

A wonderful thing happened to me three years ago. Brother Escar Tharp, pastor of the Mt. Zion United Pentecostal Church (six miles from Hohenwald), asked us to help him as he was getting a little disabled. Thank you, Brother Tharp! The fear that I have had that I'd never be able to minister again has been overcome by your allowing me to preach and thus regain my voice so that now I can preach and sing and worship as in days gone by. Brother Tharp was a local minister from the church we built in Hohenwald, so his standards of holiness were in agreement with ours.

Younger ministers are filling the pulpits and pastoring the saints that God permitted us to have a part in bringing to God. We do not regret the hard work and privation we endured with practically no salary. The great Record-keeper has that all down.

Please let me make one request in closing. Young pastors, will you please guide the children whom older ministers brought to the Lord in the way in which they were taught in the beginning. If it took a life of dedication to build a work for God, it will surely take the same dedication and consecration to keep it in proper alignment with the Lord.

We have retired from the everyday work force, but there's a calling that will never be stilled and a promise from God that will always last. I suppose I feel somewhat like the old retired horse that had raced across town pulling the fire engine. This had been his life for so many years that when the fire whistle sounded, he immediately placed himself in position for take off. Years passed. More modern equipment was being used, and now "Old Dobbin" was given the privilege to take it easy at pasture. It didn't work that way. When the whistle blew, he ran to the barn ready to be harnessed and race to the fire!

I realize that physically I've lost some of my strength and motivation, but not the call! "For the gifts and calling of God are without repentance" (Romans 11:29). "For all the promises of God in him are yea, and in him Amen, unto the glory of God by us" (II Corinthians 1:20).

by Lela Holland

Lela Chumney Holland

The Holland family, 1946

Lela Holland's Sunday school class, Hohenwald, 1949

Brother Luther honoring Hollands at Hohenwald UPC

Carlos and Lela Holland, 1985

CHAPTER Ten

Eva Hunt

In eastern Fayette County, Illinois, near St. Elmo on July 27, 1902, God blessed the humble home of Charles and Martha Fair with twin daughters, Eva Juanita and Eva Valieta who became known as Evie. Although the twins were born on a bright summer day, clouds of future sorrow loomed on the horizon. When their mother was stricken with tuberculosis, the nine-year-old twins attended school and assumed most of the household duties including cooking meals, baking bread, and mothering two younger brothers. This rigorous schedule built in the girls a moral fiber that produced women of outstanding character. Although terminally ill, the concerned mother whispered warnings to her daughters against the ways of the world.

One April morning in 1913, Martha Fair bade a final farewell to her eleven-year-old daughters and two younger sons, leaving them in the hands of a good God and a concerned father. At that time Evie was also bedfast with double pneumonia and eight abscesses in her side.

Charles called the doctor. When the doctor arrived, he told Charles, "Your daughter probably will not live, but here is some medication that may help."

Eva took care of Evie, changing the bandages on the abscesses along with her daily household duties while attending Cumberland School. Although Charles Fair had to work away from home for long hours each day, he and Eva held the family together.

Two years after the death of Martha Fair, a wealthy Methodist lady, Madge Smith from Brownstown, came to visit the Fair twins. Well known for her personal work in the Methodist church, Mrs. Smith had heard of the plight of the Fair family and came to invite them to Easter services. She bought each of the girls Easter hats and a beautiful gold-bound New Testament.

The invalid Evie read the New Testament daily and found words full of hope and healing. One day while reading her Bible, faith rose in her heart, and she felt the healing power of God. She rose from her bed and began to worship the Lord.

In her enthusiasm and faith, she burned all her medicine. Then she told her sister, "I am healed. Jesus Christ is my Healer." Concerned Eva called her father. When Charles arrived home, he said, "It's hard for me to believe you have been instantly healed. I'm calling the doctor." When the doctor arrived, he examined Evie closely and said, "This girl has been completely healed."

Evie began to walk over a mile a day to the neighbors' homes, telling them about the healing power of God. At age eighteen, Evie felt her call to preach and became a minister in the Church of God, Anderson, Indiana. She went all over the countryside preaching.

Meanwhile, on September 22, 1918, Eva married Ray Hunt in St. Louis, Missouri. Despite her sister's miraculous healing, Eva still had not given her heart to God.

Evie Fair went to Daniel Boone, Kentucky, to hold a tent revival. A terrible storm blew the tent down, and again Evie was stricken with double pneumonia. She did not want to call a doctor but tried to trust God for her healing. Before her death, God showed Evie that He was going to save her twenty-two-year-old twin sister.

One night in 1927, at age twenty-five, Eva Hunt went to the Pentecostal church in Vandalia, Illinois, where Brother A. Varnell was pastor. That night Eva Hunt received the gospel message and was baptized in the wonderful name of Jesus.

In 1929 Sister Hunt and her husband moved to Decatur, Illinois. There at Bethel Temple she heard Brother Homer White preach about receiving the Holy Ghost with the evidence of speaking in tongues. (According to Brother Thomas Suey, Brother White was the second person to be baptized in Jesus' name east of the Mississippi River. Brother G. T. Haywood was the first.) For seven consecutive nights Sister Hunt earnestly sought the gift of the Holy Ghost, and on the seventh night she was gloriously filled.

For seven years Sister Hunt labored faithfully under Brother White's leadership as a Sunday school teacher, personal worker, song leader, and young people's leader. She gave sermonettes but felt inadequate to go into full-time ministry. She had no chance to go to Bible school and had only an eighth-grade education. On the other hand, the evidence of her calling was overwhelming. As many as fourteen at one service were filled with the Holy

Ghost and baptized in Jesus' name in her classes and youth services.

Brother Casey in Bloomington, Illinois, asked her to preach at a young people's rally at his church. This was her first public sermon, but she still felt unworthy to be called a preacher.

In 1933, Sister Nora Baker of Sullivan, Illinois, asked Sister Hunt to hold a revival for her. Before the revival started, Sister Hunt laid a fleece before the Lord about her calling. "Lord, don't let a soul be saved unless You are calling me to preach." The first night of the revival eight souls came to the altar and repented. After that first night she said, "I knew I was doomed—called to preach the gospel."

As she departed from Sister Baker's church, Sister Hunt knew beyond doubt that she was called to preach. Before her lay the white field of unharvested souls. Tears for lost souls became her meat for days and nights, even years, as she became a pioneer for Pentecost in central Illinois.

In the 1930s during the Great Depression, Brother White's congregation was unable to meet the monthly payments on their church and lost their building. At this time only a few members were left, so they moved into another building where a group of African-Americans were meeting. Discouraged, Brother White thought, "Perhaps I should just disband the church." Sister Hunt began to pray. One night while she slept, the Lord spoke to her, "Redeem! Redeem! Redeem!" When she awoke, she could not understand what the message meant. Finally, after prayer, she realized that God was telling her to redeem Brother White's church. "I don't have any money, Lord, but I'll try to redeem the church."

The next day Sister Hunt asked a friend to go with her to ask the real estate agent, "Is Bethel Temple for sale? I want to redeem it." The broker told her the amount of money needed to redeem Bethel Temple and gave them a written plan: $300 down in thirty days and $20 per month.

"How can we raise that much money?" her friend asked.

"We will meet every day and fast our lunch then go to various businesses and ask for money to redeem the church," Sister Hunt replied.

The first week they raised $280 and took it to Brother White who said, "You only have to raise $20 more." The next Sunday morning Brother White and his congregation moved back into their building.

"Redeem" became a key word in her ministry. She redeemed Pentecostal churches in central Illinois: Pana, Shelbyville, Nokomis, Oak Valley, Ramsey, Witt, Taylorville, Greenleaf, and Herrick.

At this time Sister Hunt, a young businesswoman, was climbing the ladder of success in the insurance company for which she worked. They appointed her as district manager. But God spoke to her, "Go to Pana." Although she resigned her position, the insurance business had taught her two principles: how to meet the public and the importance of preparing for the future.

On Saturday afternoon, June 6, 1941, Sister Hunt arrived in Pana at Wilbur Denton's used furniture store and asked, "Are there any Pentecostals in town?"

"There's a prayer meeting in a house on Walnut Street going on now," he answered.

She walked into the meeting but was shocked to see tobacco juice dripping from the mouths of praying men and women.

The minister of the group asked, "Are you a preacher?" Then he asked if she would hold a meeting for them. "You will have to find a place to have the meeting yourself," he told her.

"I hardly think that is my responsibility," she replied.

When she returned the next Saturday, the seats had been moved to the Browns' residence. "You can hold a meeting on our front porch," Mrs. Clint Brown offered. So Sister Hunt held her first meeting in Pana. A table on the front porch served as a pulpit, and seats for the congregation were placed in the front yard. Eight men came to the porch altar for prayer after the sermon.

Until cool weather Eva Hunt preached on the Browns' front porch to her outdoor congregation. Clint and Mae Brown and Howard and Geneva Sims were in this original group. During the winter they moved inside the Browns' house.

Later someone suggested, "We might be able to hold services in the American Legion hall."

When she asked the man in charge, he said, "You'll have to okay it with the Baptist pastor next door."

The Baptist pastor said, "I think the town is big enough for both churches." So they rented the building for $3 a week, which paid the janitorial services. Sister Hunt's salary for the first year was only $20.

Enthusiastic about the possibilities for Pentecost in Pana, Sister Hunt was dismayed to learn that Pentecost did not have a good reputation in that community. Previous Pentecostals had left unpaid bills. The new pastor immediately paid all outstanding debts of the former Pentecostals. She taught and lived a life separated from the world.

One man told everyone in the community how Sister Hunt had paid a debt that earlier Pentecostals had owed him for ten years. Because of this, Sister Hunt was able to get credit, and a basement church was built.

Brother Kenneth V. Reeves preached the first revival. Thirty-five were baptized in Jesus' name and several were filled with the Holy Ghost.

Soon Brother J. H. Reeter from Vandalia asked Sister Hunt to join the Pentecostal Church Inc., which she did. Later she was officially ordained as a minister of the gospel and her church was called the Full Gospel Church.

From the front porch of Clint Brown's home on Jefferson Street to the corner of Orange and Franklin, the congregation grew into a thriving and lasting organism. Evangelists, pastors, pastors' wives, and personal workers came from this congregation to work in the harvest fields. Howard and Geneva Sims were faithful saints, and he served as Sunday school superintendent for nineteen years. Sister Sims served as Ladies Auxiliary president for twenty-eight years as well as teaching the primary Sunday school children.

In 1946 the superstructure of the Full Gospel Church was completed, and on December 4, 1966, the mortgage was burned. On the twenty-fifth anniversary of the church, Brother S. W. Chambers preached and Brother M. J. Wolff served as master of ceremonies.

The ministry of Sister Hunt and the Full Gospel Church spread over the city of Pana and surrounding towns like an umbrella. The church and its pastor gained status in the community unsurpassed by denominational churches. Businessmen, lawyers, doctors, and others greeted Sister Hunt on the street and in business places as Reverend Mrs. Hunt.

In November 1963 at the assassination of President John F. Kennedy, the Pana Ministerial Association selected Sister Hunt to preach the memorial sermon in honor of the dead president at the Pana Senior High School auditorium to a capacity crowd. The following year she received a color portrait of President Kennedy autographed by his widow, Jacqueline Kennedy, plus a personal letter of thanks by Mrs. Kennedy.

In 1947 Reverend Evangeline Davis, a Nazarene evangelist, came into contact with Pentecost under Sister Hunt's ministry. Although skeptical, Reverend Davis attended some tent meetings sponsored by the Pentecostal church but remained defensive toward her Nazarene doctrine. Then she attended a district conference in Pinckneyville with Sister Hunt, where subsequently she was baptized by Reverend J. H. Reeter. Although she did not receive the Holy Ghost at her water baptism, Sister Davis was greatly moved by the power of the name of Jesus. She shouted herself right out of the baptistery, through the church, and down the street! It was amusing to hear Sister Hunt tell of Sister Davis's baptism because of her height and Brother Reeter's short stature.

Weeks later Brother M. J. Wolff asked Sister Hunt to contact Sister Davis and request that she preach the next scheduled Herrick fellowship meeting. At this meeting, Sister Davis preached the evening message, gave the altar call, and then found her own way to a Pentecostal altar.

She had been convicted of the necessity of the baptism of the Holy Ghost while she was preaching. At that altar she received the baptism of the Holy Ghost speaking in tongues. Later Sister Davis held a revival meeting for the Pana church. From there she traveled the revival circuit throughout the United Pentecostal Church and pastored in Lonoke, Arkansas, and Columbus, Ohio. Sister Hunt had led another faithful worker into Pentecost.

During the same year, Reverend William Suey, a Free Methodist minister, came into Pentecost under Sister Hunt. When he left the Free Methodist church, several men and women in his Sunday school class followed him. Among those who followed him were Sybil Eagan, whose son labors in the United Pentecostal church in Champaign, Illinois, under the pastorate of Reverend C. Dale Sims, son of Howard and Geneva Sims. Also from Brother Suey's Sunday school class came Marguerite Keifling, whose son and daughter-in-law, Reverend and Mrs. Charles Keifling (former Virginia Estopy from Brother Branding's church in St. Louis) now pastor in Canada.

Sister Hunt firmly believed in knocking on doors, praying, fasting, visiting the sick, ministering to the poor, and preaching in jails. She knew what it was to enclose herself in a basement Sunday school room fasting and praying three days at a time. By going door to door, Sister Hunt's ministry has produced other fruitful ministries. One of these ministries is Reverend and Mrs. Orville Denton, pastor of Oak Valley UPC for twenty-five years. Sister Denton (Geneva I. Sims) was one of the children present at the Jefferson Street home mission. Also in the ministry are Brother and Sister Gerald Musser of

Mesquite, Texas, whom she won to the Lord through their children. Sister Hunt strongly emphasized children's ministries.

As she preached from the front porch of Jefferson Street, the next-door neighbor, Clarence Bland, busily stacked empty beer cans whose contents had worked havoc in his lost soul. As Mr. Bland listened to Sister Hunt preach, little did he realize that the gospel net was drawing him to the Lord. Clarence Bland ultimately became Brother Bland, who served faithfully on the board of trustees of the Full Gospel Church. At the untimely death of his young wife, Brother Bland was left with two small children. Later Clarence married Ida Mae Sims, one of the children who had been present at the first Saturday morning meeting. This was the first wedding that Sister Hunt had performed. To this union were born seven Bland children. God literally raised Brother Bland out of poverty as he established the Bland Construction Company and later developed many housing subdivisions and businesses in Illinois including Lake Lawn Motel Complex in Pana.

In 1951 Sister Hunt heard that the Oak Valley Pentecostal Church was to be razed. Alarmed, she phoned Brother M. J. Wolff, who readily set out with Sister Hunt to redeem Oak Valley. The battle was not easy, but under the direction of Brother Wolff and Sister Hunt, three unbelievers agreed to temporarily serve on the board of trustees of the Oak Valley Church because they wanted it to remain in the community. At the first service under the trees, Sister Hunt preached to over fifty men, women, and children who heard the Holy Ghost message. Brother Wolff and Sister Hunt were delighted at the fruit of their labors. The author recalls attending church services in the Oak Valley Church as his father preached by the light of kerosene lamps. From this lowly beginning came a thriving church pastored by Reverend and Mrs. Orville Denton from the Pana church. In 1941 Sister Hunt had called at the home of Brother Denton's parents (his mother was wheelchair bound) and found Orville as a young man and his sister, Myrtle Denton Sims, hungry for the Lord. Wonderful saints, the Dentons worked in the Oak Valley Church and later in the Nokomis church for over twenty-five years.

In 1943, led by the Holy Ghost, Sister Hunt went to Shelbyville, Illinois, to the home of Mr. Charles Sims to hold a prayer meeting. Sister Sims already had the Holy Ghost, but there was no Pentecostal church in town. After Sister Sims opened her home to the prayer meetings led by Sister Hunt, several Nazarenes came to receive the Pentecostal message. Needing a building, Sister Hunt and her new congregation bought and remodeled an old tavern. Some men had agreed to come and tear down the partitions, but Sister Hunt and Sister Sims wearied of waiting and tore down the partitions themselves.

Two families from the Shelbyville area, Albert and Edith Bafford and Dwayne and Naomi Ripley, had attended the church in Pana. The Bafford's nine-year-old son had witnessed to his school principal, Dwayne Ripley, and his schoolteacher, Naomi Ripley. As a result of the testimony of their faithful, persistent pupil, the Ripleys felt convicted. First Sister Ripley was filled with the Holy Ghost and baptized in Jesus' name; her husband, Dwayne, soon followed. Because the church baptistery was not filled with water, Sister Hunt took him to Vandalia to Brother Reeter's for baptism only to find that baptistery also empty. From there they drove to Ford's pond for the service, a little dampening experience for the principal's Presbyterian pride! Never discount the witness of small children. From the Pana and Shelbyville churches, the Ripleys relocated to serve in the Christian school at Calvary Tabernacle in Indianapolis pastored by Brother Nathaniel Urshan.

The Shelbyville work progressed. The old tavern was torn down and a tent set up for a revival meeting with Brother Kenneth Reeves. Ten people were baptized. Within four years Sister Hunt and the Shelbyville congregation erected a small church, and another town had a Pentecostal church.

In 1950 Sister Hunt and Sister Marguerite Keifling went to Lakewood, Illinois, to establish another church. After she had left the Pana Free Methodist Church in 1949, Sister Keifling had witnessed to her mother, Hilda Cole, about the Holy Ghost. Sister Cole, who lived in Lakewood, wanted a church built there. South of Lakewood, Sister Cole, her mother, and Sister Hunt found an abandoned school. As the three ladies entered the old building, the power of the Holy Ghost struck them to their knees in prayer and praise. "This is the place!" they knew. They purchased the building, and within a few weeks, the Sunday school attendance rose to thirty-five. Although the church is now defunct, the author remembers attending services there at Greenleaf Pentecostal Church as a small boy when his father ministered there.

In the early 1950s the Pana congregation with its home missions spirit reached out to the Taylorville Pentecostal Church pastored by Brother Kellogg. They sent a crew of men to build Sunday school rooms and helped them to obtain a loan from a savings and loan company for a parsonage.

In the late 1940s Sister Hunt went to Nokomis, Illinois, to begin another Pentecostal work. She rented a room at the library and opened the church with more than twenty people. For two or three months Sister Hunt pastored this congregation. Several people were baptized. However, the work was short-lived, and most of the Nokomis saints transferred to Pana since Sister Hunt found it too difficult to pastor both congregations. From the Nokomis church came Brother and Sister Carl Sanders. He served faithfully on the board of trustees of the Pana church for many years.

Again in the 1950s Sister Hunt was called to "redeem" a new work in Ramsey, Illinois. A Sister McNear had begun building a block structure in Ramsey but had to abandon her efforts. She contacted Sister Hunt and her young people who led the work for over a year, raising money and finishing the building. Many souls were won to the Lord. At that time, Sister Hunt brought Brother Karr from Vernon, Illinois, to pastor the new church. He labored faithfully for many years in Ramsey, and today a thriving church exists there.

Sister Hunt always worked well with her district superintendent, Brother M. J. Wolff. The Wolffs were frequent guests in the Pana church. The author remembers Brother Wolff preaching a two-hour sermon entitled "Vessels Don't Talk Back." He held the congregation in rapt attention that Sunday night. Those were days of hard, difficult battles but great spiritual victories!

In August 1967 Sister Hunt, weakened by months of

ill health, retired from the Pana Full Gospel Church after twenty-eight years of pastoring, and Brother Arlie Mulvaney, presbyter of section five and pastor of the Farina church, was called to succeed her.

After eighteen months of recuperation, Sister Hunt found retirement unsuitable. She went to Witt, Illinois, and raised $1500 to purchase the Assembly of God church building. Sister Hunt and her husband, Ray, renovated the building and established a good name for Pentecost in Witt. Within months a small but growing work was established. Ray Hunt became ill, so Sister Hunt turned the church in Witt over to Sister Marie Hagen from Effingham, Illinois.

In May 1972, Sister Hunt was called to redeem the languishing church in Herrick, Illinois, where services had dwindled to Sunday mornings only. On that first Sunday in May 1972, nine people were present. Immediately Sister Hunt and Brother Harold Pope began a renovation program. The north wall of a four-wall structure was collapsing and windows were broken. The sight was disappointing to say the least. But now in her seventies, Sister Hunt saw potential possibilities. Her eye of faith was not dimmed nor her strength abated.

The little congregation immediately began to grow. Rooms were added, the parking lot expanded, and bathroom facilities modernized. People received the Holy Ghost and were baptized in Jesus' name during ordinary services. During the summer of 1975, Sister Hunt asked the author to assist her in preaching on Sunday nights. In the fall of 1972, the author and his wife (Deborah Smithson) had been called to work in the church music department in Herrick from Brother L. H. Hardwick's church in Nashville, Tennessee. The author had grown up under the ministry of Sister Hunt as a small boy.

Sister Hunt's influence reached far. In January 1972 she taught the Bible classes during the absence of Sister S. G. Norris, wife of the president of Apostolic Bible Institute in St. Paul, Minnesota.

By the popular vote of the people of Pana, Sister Hunt was named the grand marshal of the Pana Labor Day parade. She was chosen by the community on the basis of being the person who had done the most for her community.

Sister Hunt retired from her eighth pastorate on October 22, 1977. She preached her farewell sermon, "I Don't Regret a Mile I Traveled for the Lord," to a capacity crowd.

Sister Hunt has always enjoyed and worked faithfully with organizational efforts. While she served under Reverend Homer White in the Decatur church, she was youth secretary of the Illinois District of the Pentecostal Assemblies of Jesus Christ. She also served in section five for many years as secretary of that section as well as Ladies Auxiliary president. She attended the first Illinois district camp meeting.

She was also at Murphysboro at the first youth camp. Her church took several carloads of teens to the camp. What great joy she felt at the sight of young people worshiping in the youth camps. There was something about that Holy Ghost seedbed that spawned many future preachers and workers at the old Murphysboro camp. The campgrounds were hot and humid and living conditions poor, but the sacrifice was little compared to the blessings. In the early 1950s Sister Hunt taught children's classes while the adults enjoyed the camp meeting. In 1958 she wrote curriculum for the teens she taught. Her consistent walk with God was a shining testimony to the Murphysboro campers.

Grief and sorrow have been frequent visitors in the life of Eva Hunt. Her mother died after a lengthy illness when Eva and her twin sister were only eleven. In June 1926 her father, Charles Fair, passed away on the day her twin sister, Evie V., was to be married. The wedding was postponed to a later date. In September 1926 the newly married Evie V. was holding a tent meeting in Kentucky only to have the tent destroyed in a storm. Evie V. contracted pneumonia as a result of the storm and died within a week. One Sunday night, June 4, 1966, while Sister Eva Hunt was preaching, she received a phone call. Her only granddaughter, Sue Hunt, was lying comatose in a Terre Haute hospital as a result of a bicycle accident. Sue, soon to graduate as a Registered Nurse, died twenty-five days later, never having regained consciousness. Sister Hunt's only son died unexpectedly on June 1, 1970, at age forty-seven. Her husband, Ray Hunt, died the following year on April 23.

Sister Hunt celebrated her eightieth birthday on July 27, 1982, still faithfully working in soulwinning and attending church in Herrick. What a joy to reflect on the hundreds of people she baptized, married, counseled, and dedicated as babies as well as those who received the Holy Ghost and were called to the ministry. These included Charles Kiefling, Canada; Geneva Davis, Lonoke, Arkansas; Gerald and Gladys Musser, Mesquite, Texas; Lillian Hedges, Monteagle, Tennessee; Dale Sims, Champaign, Illinois; George McCaslin, Princeton, Illinois;

Kenton Griffin (deceased); Mark Morris, Missouri; Orville Denton, Pana, Illinois; Naomi Ripley (deceased) and Thomas Suey, Herrick, Illinois.

"Redeem" was the key word the Lord spoke to Sister Hunt in the 1930s and remained the key word in her life and ministry.

Brother Thomas Suey adds a closing note.

On April 19, 1995, the day of the Oklahoma City bombing, we were called to Sister Hunt's bedside. The attending physician had said that she would soon be passing.

Shortly after seven o'clock in the evening, Sister Hunt departed this life at the age of ninety-two, only to hear the Lord say, "Well done, good and faithful servant; . . . enter thou into the joy of thy Lord."

Sister Hunt has left us all a great legacy that has taught us how to love people and win them to Jesus Christ. Her soulwinning skills were unparalleled, and that same art of disciple-making skill still lives in the hearts of her many converts and pastors whom she trained in the ministry. Having learned from Reverend Eva Hunt has only made us all richer in the Lord. Without her legacy of love, the apostolic church would not have the impact nor stability that it now enjoys in central Illinois.

by Mary Wallace and Thomas Suey

Eva Hunt, 1943

Eva Hunt, 1947

Eva Hunt, 1951

CHAPTER Eleven

Ella Lee Donaldson Kilgore

Long, long be my heart with such memories fill'd!
Like the vase in which roses have once been distill'd;
You may break, you may shatter the vase if you will,
But the scent of the roses will hang 'round it still.
—Thomas Moore

Although Ella Lee Donaldson Kilgore, my mother, died over twenty-five years ago, I still remember her well. She was so unique that I still feel her impact in my life even though she has not touched me physically for many years. Yet, when I describe her to my friends and my family, I must admit that she often appears a trifle ordinary.

Then why, I ponder in the middle of the night, does the scent of Mother's memory linger so heavily this many years after her death? And why, I ask, are tough men and strong women often driven to their knees after listening to the accountings of her spiritual experiences and her life as one of the pioneers in Pentecostal history? I'm not sure I can adequately explain her uniqueness or that I can tell her story vividly enough to allow her life to radiate through the printed words. But I will try.

Some of the stories I will tell about Mother obviously happened when I was too young to remember all the details; however, those stories will be woven as accurately as possible. I personally witnessed many beautiful and wonderful events, and those are the stories I love to tell.

My Mother

Ella Lee Donaldson Kilgore, almost five feet four inches tall, was just a little plump according to today's fashion editors. However, she was just right according to my daddy, her greatest admirer. Her hair was golden blond, and Daddy often recalled that fact with great pride as he lovingly spoke of their youthful days together. I don't personally remember seeing her with blond hair; I only remember it as soft honey brown. It was either combed into a simple bun held securely at the back of her neck with long metal hairpins, or it hung down her back in a braid at bedtime.

Mother was a country woman, and, as such, she dressed like a country woman. She wore simple dresses of black and white or navy and white. The cotton, home-made dresses were almost always high-necked, long-sleeved, and ankle length. She was so modest that she would not have considered wearing a low-cut dress. Furthermore, she would not have rolled up her wrist-length sleeves more than one or two rolls. Her sleeves always stayed securely below her elbows even when the thermometer registered a hot 90° and the humidity caused sweat to gather in small beads on her upper lip.

Along with high necklines and long sleeves, most of Mother's dresses were so long that they softly brushed against her ankles. Looking back, I just have to wonder why she wore her dresses so long. Her lisle stockings (heavy, cotton hose) were so thick that I'm sure a mosquito would have gotten discouraged trying to find an uncovered spot on which to land. But in her opinion, a lady just didn't show much leg. Even when fashion editors successfully lowered the necklines, shortened the sleeves, and raised the hemlines, Mother changed her style of dressing very little. She remained a simple, ordinary woman.

She sounds quite ordinary, doesn't she? Obviously, her uniqueness didn't come about because of any outstanding outer beauty. She had an inner beauty, however, that radiated past the simple look of the country woman—that is what made her so unique.

Early Days—Early Beginnings

There were six of us Kilgores at home in the early 1900s: Daddy; Mother; R. G., my older brother; Odetta, my older sister; Claude, Jr., my younger brother; and me. Omeda, Elizabeth, James, and Joe were added to our family later.

Home was a simple, two-bedroom cabin that humbly boasted of screenless windows, splintery floors, unpainted walls, orange-crate cabinets, and a wood-burning stove. We didn't have an indoor bathroom, hot or cold running water, an air-conditioning unit, or a gas furnace. In spite of the lack of modern conveniences, those two rooms were home for the Kilgore clan, and the people who occupied those two rooms loved each other dearly.

Every spring Mother planted a garden, and after weeks of hoeing, spading, and watering, she harvested her crop. After her crop was harvested, she spent days over her hot, wood-burning stove canning food for her family. When winter blew its chilly breath across her garden, freezing everything it breathed on, the Kilgores had no worries about food. They never went hungry because Mother's orange-crate cupboards and cellar were well stocked.

Daddy was a crane operator. He was a hard worker, and he provided for his family well. Those were good days for the Kilgores, days that would be remembered by all of us as being a time when we had all we wanted to eat, were able to sleep in our own beds each night, and were able to attend an entire school term.

Mother's Call

In the early 1920s, thousands of Americans were trying desperately to decide if they wanted Warren G. Harding or Woodrow Wilson as President of the United States. My parents were also in the throes of decision making. I don't think, however, that they were too caught up in politics at that time. I am sure that their primary concerns were not over who would be the twenty-ninth president or if the League of Nations should be an integral part of the treaties of peace. No, they were wrestling with a decision about their own personal future: a decision that ultimately affected their lives, their children's lives, and Pentecostal history.

Strange as it may seem, my parents weren't struggling over Daddy's call into the ministry or even if he should evangelize. Those two issues were settled when he accepted his call into the ministry. No, the decision they were struggling with was whether Daddy should evangel-ize alone or take his family with him. They understood that either decision would cause some heartache.

If Mother stayed at home with us children, Daddy would be away from us for long periods of time. However, even though we would miss him very much when he trav-eled, staying at home meant we children would be able to go to one school together, and we would be allowed to remain in our home. On the other hand, if the family trav-eled with him, we would be together as a family, but we would have no home of our own. Thus, that decision would force us to live in other people's homes, people we had never met.

For days my parents agonized with God in their prayers. They felt they just couldn't make any decision without first communicating with Him because they wanted to do what was right.

After days of fasting and praying and seeking God for His will, they finally decided that it would be best if Daddy traveled by himself. Mother would remain behind and care for us children.

The decision for us to stay at home seemed right for a few days; however, it wasn't long before Mother began feeling troubled by sending Daddy off by himself. She knew in her heart that she was capable of staying behind and that he was able to travel by himself. She also knew that she and we children would fare well while her hus-band was gone, but her heart kept telling her that there was something wrong with their decision.

Urgently driven by the stirring in her heart, Mother went once again to God in prayer. She humbly explained to Him that her decision to stay behind was not made because she was rebellious or stubborn. In fact, she further explained, she thought her absence obviously would not be felt as she had never sung a special at church or preached a sermon behind a pulpit. In prayer she told God that she was willing to do whatever He asked of her regardless of how small or insignificant that task seemed, but she needed to be at peace with their decision.

Somewhere deep within her, Mother knew that staying at home would be easier on her and us children. On the other hand, her instincts told her that if she stayed at home, Daddy would not be so content to stay away. Thus, if he came home when he should have been preaching, there would be sinners who would never get a chance to hear the message of the saving power of Jesus if she stayed behind. What a battle!

As she wrestled with God that memorable day so many years ago, she cried that Jesus would give her grace never to complain, no matter what she faced. As she earnestly sought His will, God communed with Mother in a very special way. I don't know if He spoke aloud to her or not. Perhaps He simply impressed a verse of Scripture on her heart, or perhaps she felt a unique calmness in her soul. She never told us how she received God's message. I only know that when we quietly entered the room where she had been praying, her face shined with a glow—a glow that only comes when the heart of a man or a woman communes with God in a very special way.

After we had finished with our dinner that evening, Mother quietly told us that God had called her to be Daddy's helpmate (such an old-fashioned word!); and as his helpmate, she would travel with him.

Later, when I was an adult, I understood that Mother had communicated that day with God in a way few are ever privileged to know because that level of communication is never reached in a moment of silent prayer or a now-I-lay-me-down-to-sleep recitation. It is made possible only when a man or a woman is willing to seek earnestly for an answer, and, more importantly, willing to wait for an answer even if it takes all day or even if it takes all day and all night.

A Helpmate

Little did Mother realize that memorable day she accepted the call of God on her life to be my daddy's helpmate what the future held for her. I am certain she could not have understood the full impact that her decision would have on the lives of her family. Some learning only comes with experience.

Mother could not have known that day she communicated with God in such a special way that she and Daddy would never own their own home, not even when they grew old. She would not have known that her children would eat most of their meals at the table of strangers and go hungry because of their fear of asking for more food. Nor could she have known that her family's education would be constantly interrupted because of their moving from city to city, a sad fact that created tremendous stress for the shyer Kilgore children.

I sincerely believe that even if Mother had fully understood the consequences of her decision to follow Daddy or had known in advance all the heartaches her family would be forced to endure, she would have considered her sacrifice nothing compared to the supreme sacrifice

Christ had made for her at Calvary. Thus, in the light of Christ's sacrifice for her, it wasn't so hard for her to quietly watch the new owners take her furniture away. She was committed to traveling with her husband so he could preach the gospel he loved so much, and she was committed to be his helpmate. That commitment made it easier for her to carefully pack her meager belongings without complaint into boxes that would later line the sides of the borrowed hack that took them to the town of Friendship.

Friendship Didn't Like Holy Rollers

The Kilgore clan must have been a sore sight that spring day as we limped into Friendship, Arkansas. We must have surely looked like a pack of rabbits stuffed into a small cage on the way to market. Imagine four rumpled, dirty kids eagerly hanging over the sides of Uncle Shorty's hack. Daddy was wiping sweat from his brow, tired from the long hard trip. Mother was exhausted and weary yet patiently waiting for us to reach our destination.

The first phase of my parents' commitment to serve Christ, selling the furniture and moving to Friendship, had been relatively simple. The next phases, however, were much more difficult. We had no home. Where would we live while we were evangelizing? We had no car or buggy or wagon. How would we travel from city to city?

Not only did my parents have concern over a place for their family to live, they had no place to have church. There was no money to rent a storefront or a community building, and no one would allow them to hold services in any of the existing church buildings. Those conditions would be enough to stop most of us today from venturing into the unknown. Yet time and time again, Daddy and Mother stretched their faith. They always believed that their needs would be supplied.

Even though they sincerely believed that their needs would be supplied, my daddy believed in putting works with his faith. Thus, once we were settled in Friendship, we began working. Every day at noon all of us walked down to the center of the town, stood on the porch front of the grocery store, and prayed out loud for the people of the community. Obviously the people didn't like us praying out loud for them, but we kept on praying and witnessing anyway.

Then, according to their faith, a man gave an acre of ground. That was just enough land to build an open shed, not an elaborate place, but somewhere for the few believers to meet and worship God.

Once the question of a church building was settled, it wasn't long until the questions of housing and transportation were answered also. Daddy's cousin allowed us to move into a small shack that sat in the middle of a cotton patch. I don't remember how, but somehow Daddy arranged for transportation.

Soon Daddy started preaching, telling his favorite stories of how God had saved him from a life of sin. However, he quickly discovered that the townspeople of Friendship did not want to hear his story of how God had so graciously filled him with the Holy Ghost.

Today it's rather common for people to speak openly about their unique experiences of speaking in tongues with few fears of rejection. In fact, speaking in tongues is a common experience now. Many religious organizations

179

who do not recognize the experience as being essential to salvation make a place in their congregations for the charismatics—a kind word that replaces the old phrase "the tongue talkers." This was not the case in Friendship during the early 1900s.

We had not been in Friendship long before we felt the full impact of the townspeople's hostility. Sometimes an angry person would hurl a rotten egg at Daddy, splattering the yolk all over his freshly ironed shirt. Others would shout obscenities at him while he preached, causing him to blush in shame that his family was forced to endure such language.

Then there were times when the grown men were too cowardly to attack the preacher, so they vented their anger on the younger members of the preacher's family—children too small to retaliate. My stomach still churns when I recall the day my brother, R. G., stumbled onto our porch, carefully holding his bleeding back and crying for Mother.

"R. G., what happened to you?" Mother asked as she tenderly cradled him in her arms and gently explored the welts that covered his arms.

R. G.'s youthful voice was husky from crying. Hesitantly he told Mother the sad story that graphically explained how some people can be crazed by their prejudices and fears. When he finished, Mother continued her interrogation.

Seeking more information, she asked, "R. G., what did you do to make Mr. Sands so mad at you that he would beat you so severely?" Her tone clearly indicated that if he had been beaten by a teacher, he had surely deserved the punishment.

"I didn't do anything," R. G. answered. Salty tears filled his eyes as he remembered the senseless beating he had received in front of his classmates. "Mother, Mr. Sands doesn't hate me because of anything I did. He just hates me because Daddy is a Pentecostal preacher."

Mother still refused to believe that an adult would attack her child in such a brutal way. "Now, R. G., surely there is more to the story than that. I can't believe that he would beat you just because he hates your daddy."

"Yes, he does, Mother, he does!" he replied. A shudder ran through his youthful body causing fresh spasms of grief. "Every time he hit me, he screamed, 'I wish your family had never come to Friendship. I wish your family had never come to Friendship!'"

"Now, R. G., you build a fire in the stove, and, Odetta, you and Blanchie Fay set the table," Mother instructed. "I need to go pray for a while." As she closed the door behind her, we heard her pray for her children, her husband who was away preaching, and for the people of Friendship. After a long time, we heard her humming, "'Tis so sweet to trust in Jesus."

When she came back into the kitchen, her face was free of worry and resentment. As she quietly heaped our plates with hot cornbread and filled our bowls with homemade vegetable soup, she did so without anger, for she had made peace with God. She had made peace with the man who had so unmercifully beaten her oldest son.

That horrible day seems so long ago. I remember I did not understand what Mother was trying to tell us. My young mind was simply unable to comprehend the magnitude of the lesson she was trying so desperately to teach us. Even today I am not certain that I fully understand the full impact of forgiveness. However, when I am hurt or when I feel the need to retaliate, I still hear her say, "R. G., you must forgive Mr. Sands because he didn't know any better." I remember similar words spoken by a Man hanging from an old rugged cross many years ago. He said, "Father, forgive them; for they know not what they do" (Luke 23:34).

They Called Him Paul Ezekiel

When Paul Ezekiel was born, my parents chose a special name for their very special child. R. G., Odetta, Claude, Jr., and I had been born before their conversion. Even though they loved us dearly, Paul Ezekiel was different, for he was the first child born to them after their conversion. Thus, Daddy called him Paul after the great apostle Paul and Ezekiel after his favorite book in the Bible. We children simply called him "Little Paul."

Little Paul had the biggest, roundest eyes. When he looked at me, quietly staring as if he were trying to memorize my features, I loved him so much that I thought he was the sweetest, prettiest baby I had ever seen. He was different, too. Unlike other babies I had been around, Little Paul rarely cried or fussed or made demands. In fact, most of the time he was content to lie quietly on a pallet or a bed and wait patiently for someone to tenderly pinch his pale cheek or sing him a lullaby.

My mother treated Little Paul special, too. Most of the time she quietly rocked him and crooned simple tunes into his ears while holding him tightly to her round bosom. I think that she must have sensed, as mothers often do, that her tiny son was very fragile and that he needed lots of care.

When Little Paul was only six months old, a measles epidemic swept through our town, savagely attacking the young and innocent. The weakest, helpless victims were left not only with measles but with pneumonia as well.

First Little Paul contracted the measles. Day by day the disease ravaged his young body, leaving him weak and feverish. Then pneumonia attached itself to his weakened body, leaving him defenseless. Day by day he grew weaker.

Night after night we hovered around Little Paul, gently touching his feverish head, stroking his burning arms and crooning sweet nothings in his ears as if willing him to good health. And Mother cradled him in her arms and carefully held him when he was wracked by the coughing spasms that shook him.

After a while, Little Paul's tiny body stopping fighting. One black night he simply stopped breathing.

What words can adequately describe the death of our Little Paul? Who really understands the anguish Mother must have felt as she watched the tiny coffin being lowered into the cold, stony ground—the final resting place for her newest son?

I'm not really sure that I can describe how my mother felt that cold day as she turned from the graveside and slowly walked to the car. I was just a child myself, and she never shared her feelings with me.

We moved from Paris, Texas, a few weeks after we buried Little Paul. As we were leaving town, I asked Mother if we could go by the graveyard and see the grave before we left.

"No, Blanchie Fay," she answered. "We have a long way to drive, and remember that Little Paul is in the arms of Jesus."

All day long I listened to my mother as she sighed deep sighs of unspoken grief. Even though the tears did not fall, her sighs spoke loudly of the emptiness of her arms and the pain in her heart. Yet not one time did I hear her blame God for her loss. Neither did her problems ever cause her to say one word to discourage her husband from preaching the gospel he loved so much.

Conclusion

"Blanche," my handsome husband said, pulling me close to him and wrapping his strong arms around me, "I don't want to hurt you, but I have something to tell you. Your mother is a very sick woman."

"Oh, no," I cried, slumping against him and laying my head on his broad shoulders. "Don't tell me that she is going to die. Please, I just can't give her up." At least that is what I thought at the moment. I was consumed with grief. My sorrow was for a woman who had been such a vital part of my life.

Several months later, long hard months spent sitting quietly by her bedside, watching her slip away, I was forced to give her up—something I did not think I could ever do.

After she was buried in a lonely grave in Paris, Texas, I carefully sorted through her belongings, searching for some small keepsake that I could keep to remind me of her.

I suppose I could have chosen a dress, but I couldn't have worn it because hers would have been too outdated for me. And I could have selected one of her hats, but it would not have complemented my dresses very well. On the other hand, I could have decided on a pair of her shoes. However, they wouldn't have looked right with my more sophisticated clothes.

Finally, after a long while, I did choose one small item, one that has long been buried among the other keepsakes that I will pass along to my children. My choice was just something material that I knew would become more fragile with age. And even today, I'm certain that after I'm gone, my children will probably come across it, decide they don't want it, and throw it away. For material things are like that; they fade, become fragile, and are discarded at the whim of the owner. But memories—now they are something different! They never grow more fragile with age, nor do they lend themselves to be thrown away. No, memories are the threads that bind yesterdays and todays and tomorrows together. Memories are what cause me to cry when I think of Mother—what she was and what she might have been in today's world.

If my mother were living today, she would probably have a difficult time fitting in for she was such a simple person. Her clothes would certainly date her, and her speech would surely tell of her limited education.

However, beyond her simple dresses and limited vocabulary, if she could step into a room, when she left, those left behind would probably lean to the one nearest them and ask, "What is there about her that is different?"

And if I could, I would reply, "It's not the way she dresses or talks or walks. She has an inner beauty that shines so brightly that after being gone from me for over twenty-five years, I still feel her impact on my life."

by Mrs. F. V. Shoemake (daughter)

Brother & Sister Kilgore, 1954

CHAPTER Twelve

Minnie (Ellis) Kinzie

God has His chosen in mind continually. He has a reason for each of us. His purpose will be accomplished in His own time. Circumstances occur that move us into the place and position that He desires. Minnie Kinzie was no exception.

She was born in Bremen, Indiana, on August 13, 1872. At the time Bremen was just a small community. She spent most of her 106 years in that vicinity. She married there, gave birth to her five children there, and enjoyed the social pleasures of that locale. She was settled in to spend all of her life in that area.

But then her husband, William, decided to buy a farm near Lapaz, Indiana, and move there. She conscientiously opposed it. It was 1919 and she was reluctant to leave. Her family, friends, and the church were in Bremen. The change promised to be a hardship for her. But it was the will of God! It would take many years for it to work out, but nevertheless it did.

Their home in Bremen was comfortable. They built it

with the latest features of that day: electricity, washing machine, city water, modern kitchen, telephone, hot water heat and other amenities common to city life. A sister lived next door, and other family members were but a short distance away. Their large front porch was an evening visitation center in the summertime as many folks walked by on evening strolls. A short chat with each one was always in order.

The farm was quite different. No running water, hand-rub washing, clothes hung outside winter and summer to dry, no furnace heat, a wood-burning stove, no heat in the upstairs bedrooms, and an outhouse. In the city the school was across the street from their home. On the farm the school was a mile and a half away, necessitating the children's riding to school in a horse-drawn school-hack.

It was no wonder she was reluctant to move! She didn't spend the first winter there because of these inconveniences. When summer came, it wasn't so bad. The roosters crowing to announce the dawn, the clucking of the busy chickens as they scratched the ground in search of food, the mooing of the cattle, the smell of the newly-mown hay, and the kids romping in the spacious lawn soothed her anxiety. It wasn't long until she dearly loved it. Years later, when they moved back to Bremen, the adjustment was worse than when they moved to the farm.

The move was the will of God. Things happened that proved this to be true. One of them was becoming acquainted with Jennie Berger, next-door neighbor to the east. They became the best of friends although Minnie was much older than Jennie. They spent many hours studying the Bible together. It was a crucial time in the life of her dear friend. Mrs. Berger was questioning baptism in the name of Jesus Christ and receiving the Holy Ghost.

Shortly after Mrs. Berger was baptized, Minnie was also. Later both of them received the baptism of the Holy Ghost. Oneness apostolics had now invaded their neighborhood. They attended church wherever they could.

Minnie was a gracious, kind, loving, and helpful person, ready to join any endeavor to help others. During World War I, she helped clothe unfortunate Belgian children deprived of sufficient clothing because of the conflict.

She was not a leader but one who could be counted on in any legitimate endeavor.

She was a member of a denominational church in Bremen, where her parents also attended. Her grandfather donated the land the church was built on. In the country she attended a split-off of that church until she received the Holy Ghost.

She was a stalwart individual with lots of stamina. This was proven by raking her yard at the age of one hundred two, when she fell and fractured her hip. She was seventy-two when her husband passed away, and she lived thirty-four more years. In her eighties she made four trips to the West Coast—one by train, one by plane, and two by automobile.

She had an intense interest in everything her five children did as well as her many grandchildren. Her interest included sincere prayer that they would remain faithful to God.

The Bible was her constant companion. She read it every day, and when she could no longer read, listened to it on tape.

As she reached the century mark of her life, the town of Bremen was planning to celebrate its centennial. A committee was appointed to work out all the details.

"Is anyone alive," the committee members asked each other at their first meeting, "who could remember what it was like then?"

"I believe Mrs. Kinzie could," the chairman stated.

They were soon at her door seeking to interview her.

Their first question was, "Do you, Mrs. Kinzie, remember anything about Bremen when you were a child?"

"Oh, yes," she replied, "I remember many things about it."

"How large was it then?" the chairman queried.

"To the best of my memory, it was but a small community. Where my house is today was farmland. In fact farms made up most of the area then."

"How long have you lived here?" he asked.

"I was born here, lived all but twenty years here. Those twenty years we lived on a farm a few miles west of town; but Bremen was our shopping area, and we were in and out of town constantly."

"Was there a downtown area then?" he questioned.

"To me as a child, it seemed like a big downtown area, but I know now there were only a few buildings in the central part. Most of what is here now was built as I was growing up."

"What were the streets like? Were they paved then?"

"No, they were dirt, and it was somewhat later that they were paved with brick," she explained.

"Were there streetlights? I know electricity was not yet available, but did they have something else?" he questioned.

"There were lights that a lamplighter lit every evening and put out in the morning."

"The village was quite remote, would you say?" he asked.

"Very much so. Since horse and buggy was the only means of transportation, we never got very far away from town. In fact there were not many towns around here. There were the two cities of South Bend and Mishawaka, but they were twenty miles away. A person had to plan to stay overnight if he went there. And, too, the roads were dirt and often impassable, especially after a snowstorm or a heavy rain. The Baltimore and Ohio railroad went through the north side of Bremen, and one could travel east or west on it," she replied.

"When we have this celebration, Mrs. Kinzie, would you consider riding in the official car during the parade we are planning?" he questioned.

"Why, yes, if I'm able," she answered.

When the parade took place, she was in the official car along with the mayor and a couple of other officials. It was quite an honor being the only person to be as old or older than the town.

Another interesting event in her life was being a patient of Doctor Otis T. Bowen. He called her his star patient. Later, when he was elected governor of Indiana, he sent her a dozen roses in celebration of it! When he returned to Bremen during his three terms as governor, he often inquired about her welfare.

Why the account of this gracious woman? Her youngest child, Fred, met and married Vera Berger, their next-door neighbor on the farm. They became evangelists, and then pastored in Toledo, Ohio. Vera Kinzie was

191

appointed president of the Ohio District Ladies Auxiliary and later president of the Ladies Auxiliary of the United Pentecostal Church, International, for many years. They were prominent in apostolic circles, traveling throughout the States, the provinces of Canada and around the world. Fred Kinzie served as district presbyter of Ohio for twenty-five years and on general boards of the UPCI as a regional presbyter, the Harvestime Radio Commission, and the Foreign Missions Board.

by Fred and Vera Kinzie (son and daughter-in-law)

Minnie Kinzie at the age of 94.

CHAPTER Thirteen

Augusta Anderson Lundquist

"Your life is over. Your life is over." The rhythmic voices of the train wheels seemed to sing the sad words in Augusta's ears. Her heart repeated the refrain. Just a few short days ago she had been by the side of her minister husband traveling and preaching in Oregon. She loved the ministry. Everywhere she and Ed Lundquist traveled, they met people with tremendous needs and tremendous hunger. What a joy to share this Pentecostal message with them and see hope light up their eyes.

But it was over. Augusta sat alone in the passenger car of the eastbound train. She was returning to her three daughters, Fern, Genevieve, and Vivian, in St. Paul, Minnesota. Ed's body traveled behind her in the baggage car. He had suffered a massive heart attack in Salem, Oregon. Ahead lay the long journey alone.

Grief and fear tore at Augusta's heart. It was 1936 and the country was in the hungry clutches of the Great Depression. Ed and Augusta had lived a faith-walk that was dependent on the offerings they received where they ministered. Insurance was not part of the faith-walk. There was no home for Augusta. She faced an unknown future armed only with a still-burning desire to be involved in ministry.

Augusta felt alone, but she wasn't. She had committed her life to God in 1920 at a country church in South Dakota. For as long as she could remember, she had an intense hunger for God. She had listened to her immigrant father's story of how he had gone into the woods in Sweden in the mid-1800s and received an experience with God. In her 1971 autobiography to her family, Augusta told of John Anderson's experience.

"My father, John August Anderson, was reared in a home where very strict religious laws and rules of the Lutheran State Church were observed. At quite an early age he lost both his mother and father. Some relatives who lived on his father's estate in Sweden were appointed by the State Church to train and care for him and his younger brother, Alfred.

"While he was yet a young man he no doubt enjoyed the pleasures of sin, but there was a void of peace and joy in God. He often told us children how he had a desperate hunger for the reality of God. One day he heard that some meetings were being held in the woods outside the city. Out of curiosity, and maybe to have some fun, he went with some of the boys. He found people worshiping God in sincerity, happily shouting and singing and preaching the Word with a power that could save from sin.

"My father listened and was drawn to the preaching. A conviction of his sins gripped his soul, and he cried out to God in repentance for His forgiveness.

"Let me try to relate what my father told me:

'Something fell on me from heaven. All my religious rites, rules, and forms fell from me. Joy and peace filled my soul. My being was flooded with a heavenly downpour, and I knew without a doubt I was a child of God. At once I felt I must hurry home to my people. My joy was so great. It seems I was carried like Philip in the Bible. As I hurried along, I continued to speak in a language I did not know. When I arrived home I told my family about my newfound joy, but I met much resistance. They told me I had disgraced my home and the church. I was forbidden to ever attend the meetings in the woods. I had to make a decision. I felt sure I must obey God rather than man. This decision resulted in my being put out of my home, disowned, and disinherited. However, I knew I had an inheritance given to me from God!'"

Her father's words created a desire in Augusta for the same kind of experience. The heart hunger had not been met by anything in her life: her parents or her eight siblings; the childless relatives who raised her and provided a comfortable home and education; her dear husband, Ed Lundquist; or their four children; nor the denominational church they attended.

Augusta Caroline Anderson was born June 8, 1880, in Westmoreland, Sweden, to John and Anna Anderson. In 1882 John and Anna, with their oldest child, Daniel, and Augusta Caroline (age two) emigrated to America and settled near relatives in Dows, Iowa. At the age of five, Augusta made her home with John and Betty Vallin, cousins of the family. The Vallins did not have children, and because of the meager circumstances of the growing Anderson family, they opened their hearts to Augusta. She was raised as their daughter and given opportunities to fulfill her desire to be a teacher.

At age eighteen Augusta taught her first school in a Danish colony near Latimer, Iowa. She continued to teach for the next five years. Of those days Augusta wrote:

"My life thus far had been greatly involved with my teaching career: eight months of regular school session, vacation months spent at Teacher's Institute, then a special six weeks' training and teaching new immigrants from Scandinavia."

Life was soon to change, for she met Ed Lundquist. They fell in love and were married December 23, 1902. Augusta was twenty-two years old. Life seemed so good. A home was established, and they joined a denominational church. Ed supervised a meat market in Spencer, Iowa, while Augusta devoted herself to raising their four children. Then health problems created the need for a different occupation, so Ed and Augusta moved to South Dakota to farm close to Augusta's parents. Augusta continued her story:

"In the spring of that same year, Holiness people held a three-day conference in a community church in Clark, South Dakota. At this time we both realized God was calling us to repentance. We attended those three all-day meetings. That was the first step my husband made to serve the Lord. God met him at this time, and he was a changed man. Everything was changed.

"Many were stirred in this little community church. Prayer meetings were held in homes. Deep conviction from God had settled over the countryside. This was a forerunner of Pentecost—getting us ready for an outpouring of the Holy Ghost which took place in Clark later in 1920."

Ed and Augusta heard from family members of a Holy

Ghost revival that was taking place at Midway Tabernacle, St. Paul, Minnesota, where Brother William Booth-Clibborn was the pastor. Augusta wrote of what happened.

"My husband left for St. Paul to see for himself what this was all about. Special meetings were being held in Midway Tabernacle with Brother Andrew Urshan as evangelist.

"That night as my husband stepped through the door of the church, the power of God struck him. It surged through him from head to foot. Brother Urshan, while preaching, gave a message in tongues in the Swedish language. This was directly from God to my husband. The message was to receive this truth; it is from God. 'This is the way, walk ye in it' (Isaiah 30:21).

"My husband accepted this from God and was baptized in water in the name of Jesus Christ for the remission of his sins.

"He came home rejoicing, knowing without a doubt that he had received and obeyed what God had commanded Peter to preach in Acts 2:38. Sure of truth, the fire fell in our home. People over the countryside became hungry for God. Brother Booth-Clibborn sent his wife, who was also an evangelist, to come and minister to us. The revival flame of Pentecost began to burn the very first night.

"The second night as Sister Booth-Clibborn gave the altar call, I felt that desperate hunger for the reality of an assurance of being born again. In a few minutes, God was speaking through me in other tongues."

The countryside was stirred and the entire congregation of the little country church received the Pentecostal message.

Now, sixteen years later, Augusta traveled on the east-bound train headed for an unknown future. But she wasn't alone. The Lord she loved traveled with her. God's plan for her life had additional chapters for her to live out. The year was 1936. Augusta was fifty-six years old.

One year later in the fall of 1937, the door of ministry was opened for Augusta that would consume the rest of her days. Brother S. G. Norris asked her to join the faculty he was bringing together for a Bible school. Brother Norris had a divine call and a burden for the training of young ministers. The Norris family had moved in 1934 to St. Paul, Minnesota, from New York City, where Brother Norris had started a church. Now in 1937 another chapter was being written in their lives and in Augusta's. His invitation allowed the burden in Augusta's heart for continued involvement in the ministry to find its release.

How far reaching are God's preparations for our lives. In her late teens, Augusta attended Normal School in Dows, Iowa, and was trained to be a teacher. For several years she taught until she married Ed Lundquist and then devoted herself to raising their family, three daughters and one son. After Ed and Augusta had received the new-birth experience, Ed felt called to the ministry. He pastored in Spencer, Iowa, and also in Rice Lake, Wisconsin. Later he traveled as an evangelist.

Teacher, wife, mother, ministry. And again a teacher. Her education and training as a teacher when she was a young woman gave her the foundation to fulfill God's purpose for her later years at the Apostolic Bible Institute.

English and Church History were the assigned classes. Much preparation had to be given to establish the courses of study. Later Personal Evangelism, Religious

Analysis, and World Missions, as well as the ABI library, were added to Augusta's schedule. Of all the subjects she taught, World Missions became her heartbeat. This intensity remained with her until her death. She passionately viewed her calling to teach at ABI as a holy calling.

Augusta never accumulated much in possessions. She never owned a home. She lived a very frugal lifestyle, dependent on the generosity of others. But she loved what she was doing and felt she was involved in something bigger than she was. She was right. The hunger for God kept her seeking for Him until her Pentecostal experience connected her to an eternal world. She became an ordained minister of the United Pentecostal Church in 1955.

She had a favorite verse of Scripture she clung to and quoted often. "Therefore, my beloved brethren, be ye stedfast, unmoveable, always abounding in the work of the Lord, forasmuch as ye know that your labour is not in vain in the Lord" (I Corinthians 15:58).

Augusta's prayer life was evident to those who were close to her. She prayed daily for the missionary families who were serving around the world. She also kept an active correspondence with missionaries. Many of them had been her students at ABI.

Fayne Lundquist, her only living son, was not living for the Lord, and she spent much time on her knees crying out to the Lord to save him. Many times during the day she would slip away from others, and from her room the familiar sound of her prayer would be heard through the house. God is faithful. She understood that. So she prayed.

She went home to be with the Lord and her beloved Ed at the age of ninety-nine, just a few months short of the age of one hundred. She left behind an extended family of believers, many of them involved in the ministry. Their Pentecostal experiences were built on the foundation of Augusta's heart-hunger and quest for God.

She touched many lives in her quest and hunger for God.

by Carol James (granddaughter)

Augusta Anderson Lundquist at age 22, just before her marriage to Ed Lundquist

Augusta Lundquist as a Bible school teacher, 1937, age 57

CHAPTER Fourteen

Fern Lundquist Newstrand

"This is what I want!" Fern sat beside her favorite aunt and watched the young people of Midway Tabernacle in St. Paul, Minnesota. In all of her sixteen years, she had never seen young people who demonstrated such joy. She watched their fresh enthusiasm as they worshiped the Lord. It was 1920, and of all the things that the farmer's daughter from South Dakota had experienced in her visit to the big city, this place and what she was feeling were the best.

A few days later Papa came to take her back home. He had heard about this Pentecostal message and wondered about it, so Fern and Papa both went to church that day with Aunt Beda. During the preaching, the young Persian evangelist, Andrew D. Urshan, gave a message that seemed to be just for Papa.

Brother Urshan declared in Swedish: "This is the way, walk ye in it." Ed Lundquist was a son of Swedish immigrants, so the language was familiar. But the authority and power of the words from Isaiah 30:21 were not. He watched and listened and was deeply stirred.

Following the service, Papa approached Brother Urshan and spoke to him in the Swedish language. Brother Urshan explained, "I do not speak that language."

"But you spoke in the Swedish language when you were preaching," Ed replied with a puzzled expression.

"That was God speaking to you. Obey what He said," Brother Urshan commanded.

And Papa did. He was baptized in Jesus' name for the remission of his sins and received the baptism of the Holy Ghost before he and Fern returned home to South Dakota. A short while later Sister Booth-Clibborn, whose husband pastored the St. Paul church, traveled to the farming community in Clark, South Dakota, where the Lundquists lived. She preached the Pentecostal message of Acts 2:38, and the entire church received their own Pentecost. The first person to receive the Holy Ghost was Fern's mother, Augusta Lundquist.

Fern Rosella Lundquist was the first-born child of Swedish parents, Carl Edward and Augusta Caroline Lundquist. She was born in Iowa on December 20, 1903. She had three siblings, and circumstances positioned her as a strong influence in each of their lives. Each of them lived with her after she established her own home.

After her introduction to Pentecost in both Minnesota and South Dakota, Fern was able in a few months to move to St. Paul and become a part of Midway Tabernacle. She received the Holy Ghost in St. Paul. Many friendships were made among those young people who had impressed her with their love for God. She found a job at the telephone company, and later married a tall, handsome Swedish carpenter, Albert Newstrand.

Soon four beautiful children joined them on the front rows of the church. The memories of home and church are so mingled in those children today because God's house was an integral part of their lives. Honor and respect for the ministry were exampled by Albert and Fern and learned by their children. Each of the children was baptized in Jesus' name and received the Holy Ghost as children or teenagers. Each child is still serving God and involved with kingdom business.

Albert and Fern served their church with faithfulness. Albert served as church treasurer, deacon, janitor, and trustee. Fern played the piano, taught Sunday school for many years, led the weekly women's prayer group, a ladies' auxiliary group, and in her seventies was asked to teach a class of teen girls.

But the most important lessons were taught to their children. Ron, the oldest, was playing in the woods with his friends. It was fun until his stomach began to hurt. It really hurt badly and, in retrospect, was possibly an appendicitis attack. This cannot be confirmed because the family rarely went to the doctor. Ron ran home, and when Fern realized he needed more help than she could give him, she said, "I will call the pastor, and when he comes and prays for you, Jesus will heal you." When the pastor, Brother S. G. Norris, was unable to come, Sister Norris came. She prayed. God healed. Ron has never forgotten that powerful lesson he learned as a child. Jesus is our healer. Faith was planted deep in his heart that day by the simple words of Mama.

Daughter Carol remembers classic words Fern taught the women of the United Pentecostal church in Athens, Ohio, where her husband, Glen James, pastored. It was a mother-daughter luncheon, and Fern was the guest speaker. She told the women that when she was raising her four children, there had been times when she did not understand her pastor's actions. Some members of the church became angry and left the church. Fern stated with simplicity, "I could not leave. I had to trust the man of God. My children had to have the opportunity to be saved. If I left, I would remove that opportunity from them."

Fern poured herself into her family and raised the four children to love God. Raising her little flock was her greatest calling. They all remember the nightly sessions when Fern read to them. Snuggled closely to her on the brown velvet couch, they listened to Bible stories and *Pilgrim's Progress*. The nightly sessions helped build strong foundations. The children certainly did not understand all the deeper truths, but they absorbed the essence and spirit of the Word. The same was true when the children sat with Albert and Fern on the front pews of the church. When Brother Norris taught doctrine and Revelation from his charts, something wonderful happened in the spirit of the children. We must never assume that children cannot receive the ministered Word. Fern's children did. Yours will also.

We hear so much today of neglected and abused children. They certainly existed in the 1930s and 40s. Fern's children only remember security and love. Daughter Carol remembers how safe she felt as a child when Fern would take her by the hand and place her close to her as Fern joined the other women of the church family around the altar. Carol still loves the feeling of security she feels when she prays around the altar with others close by. Lingering around the altar with the church family was a frequent ending to the services and brings back sweet memories.

At every meal and at bedtime prayers, four little blond heads bowed and said their Swedish prayers together. The Swedish words were twisted and mispronounced and certainly not understood by the small children, but a discipline of prayer was being established in them.

Albert and Fern struggled as did all American families during the 1930s and 40s, for those were the days of the Great Depression and World War II. The Newstrand children have memories of their parents sharing what they had with others who were in need. The early childhood home had a railway line close to the property, and often tramps who traveled the country by rail would knock at the kitchen door. Fern could always find food to give to those men who had lost hope. Others who struggled to feed their families often left with their arms filled with groceries after visiting with the Newstrands.

A woman in the St. Paul church who had several small children asked Fern one day for advice about raising her children to love God. Fern's answer was simple: "Keep them involved in everything the church offers." One of the ways Albert and Fern kept their children involved was to introduce them to the wonderful world of music. Lessons were sacrificially planned into the budget. The not-so-pleasant squawkings of horns and clashing chords on the piano and several other instruments were endured by patient parents. All the children, playing a variety of instruments, used their music in the church orchestra. All three daughters play the organ and the piano and consider the music as a wonderful, long-lasting gift from their parents.

Ron is a United Pentecostal church minister and pastors in Newark, Ohio. He served the Ohio District UPC as district superintendent for several years. Both Mary (Rogers) and Carol (James) are United Pentecostal Church ministers' wives. Beverly (Hicks) has served the church with her gift of music.

By what standards do we judge a life to be successful? The things to which we give attention and upon which we place value are far different from God's view. We can be confident by reading His Word that faithfulness to God and His kingdom and attention to teaching our children to live for God are of greatest value. So we can judge Fern as successful. She served her family and her church for over sixty years. Her love for God and His house never diminished. She was a faithful servant until her death in Newark, Ohio, in 1984 at age eighty.

"Mama, we will never forget you and the things you taught us about God. Your love and lessons are planted deep inside of us."

"Who can find a virtuous woman? for her price is far above rubies. . . . Her children arise up, and call her blessed; her husband also, and he praiseth her. . . . A woman that feareth the LORD, she shall be praised" (Proverbs 31:10, 28, 30).

by Carol Newstrand James (daughter)

Fern Lundquist Newstrand

Fern Newstrand, age 17, in Minneapolis

Fern Newstrand at the age of 65

Albert and Fern with the "flock of four," Ron, Mary (Rogers), Carol (James) and Beverly (Hicks) (1940)

CHAPTER Fifteen

"Molly" (Imorette Rebecca) Palmer

Molly Palmer's family was numbered with the wealthy of the community. Since she was the eldest of five children, two boys and three girls, much thought was given to her education. She attended elementary school, and as soon as she was of high school age, she was sent to Kingston, the island of Jamaica's capital city, where she attended St. Simons College. There she lived with members of her father's family.

In 1942 while still at school in Kingston, Molly started having thoughts about God and living a Christian life. Plans were also in place for her to travel to England to further her education in medicine as soon as her studies in Kingston were completed.

In that same year she was invited to the Pentecostal church on Wildman Street, where she met Pastor and Mother Russell and their daughters, Maggie, Valda, and Nina. They introduced her to baptism in water, calling on the name of Jesus. Her parents, being Baptists, would not have allowed her to go there since the Pentecostal church was looked down upon.

In the summer of 1943, while traveling home on a bus from school for the holidays, Molly decided that upon her return to school, she would be baptized and live for the Lord Jesus. On reaching home she told her mother of her decision, but she was not offered any encouragement. Her parents were both more interested in her education and the prospect of her becoming a medical doctor.

When she returned to Kingston after the holidays, she again visited the church on Wildman Street and spoke to Mother Russell about her desire to be baptized in Jesus' name. At that time baptisms were performed in the sea, so she was accompanied by the pastor, other ladies, and deacons to the beach where she was baptized in the sea in the name of the Lord Jesus.

She became actively involved in the activities of the church. Each evening she would go to church. On Monday evenings, she participated in a special class held by the ladies, where they would crochet, embroidery, and do all types of sewing and craft work. On Tuesday she attended young people's service where there was much singing, praying, and Bible reading. Wednesday evening was tarrying service when those without the Holy Ghost would be prayed for, and on Thursdays she would attend Bible studies.

Not long after her parents became aware of her "rebellious" activities, which they realized no lecture could change, her father decided to stop providing for her as a result of what he called her rebellion. Even so, being a determined young lady, she trusted in the Lord Jesus Christ and continued living for Him and exercising her newfound but everlasting belief.

Going to England to pursue medical studies did not become a reality, so she joined the civil service and was employed as a clerk to the Ministry of Agriculture at Hope Gardens for many years. During that time she continued to do whatever she was called upon to do at church. She became a Sunday school teacher and also prepared presentations for seminars whenever they were planned.

In those early years of her walk with the Lord, Molly experienced His richest blessings and anointing in her life, always studying the Word of God under the guidance of Pastors A. D. Varnado, Ralph Reynolds, and Paul Reynolds.

Her friends were always deeply spiritual. She, along with her four closest friends, were always together until 1950-51, when three of them got married. Carmen, now Mrs. Stewart, an outstanding woman of God, later lost her husband, who was pastor of that organization. Another friend, Joyce Barnes, also became the wife of a bishop. She went home to be with the Lord a few years ago.

On December 26, 1951, Molly married A. Tennyson Palmer, a young man who loved God. This started them on a path to an adventurous life. During the following years, she gave birth to three children.

Molly and her husband took the Word of God very seriously and worked in unity. Molly was secretary for the national Sunday School Department, and her husband was the director. She would type, package, and distribute the lessons throughout the island each month. She was also the recording secretary for the national conferences of the United Pentecostal churches for many years.

Her husband, an insurance salesman with the Jamaica Mutual Insurance Company, received a promotion in his job. This required that he migrate to Montego Bay, St. James, in the western part of the island. Therefore they had to make plans to leave Kingston. Molly got a transfer from her job to the Agriculture Office in Irwin, St. James, and in 1961 Molly and her family moved to Montego Bay.

After settling down, they discovered that there was not a church close enough for them to worship. The nearest Pentecostal church was an hour and a half's drive away. So they started praying in earnest for direction for a solution to the problem. Their desire to have their children in Sunday school on Sundays propelled them to start a Sunday school. They went in search of a place in the densely populated community of Glendevon, where they met a Sister Graham who also had three children whom she desired to be in Sunday school. She consented for the Palmers to start a Sunday school in her home on Sunday evenings.

The Sundays following would find Molly, her husband, and their three children journeying to Glendevon for Sunday school. This continued for a time as they prayed unceasingly for God to open a way. Their great concern was for the children to be taught to worship.

One Sunday morning after prayer, Brother Palmer got into his car and drove along Albion Road for no apparent reason. While driving along, he saw a man putting up a "For Sale" sign on a lot. He got out of the car and told the man, who was the agent for the property, to take the sign down as he intended to purchase the lot. This, of course, was an act of faith and surely a command from God Himself.

When he arrived home, he said, "Come inside. Let us go and pray." Molly was in the kitchen preparing breakfast. Immediately she put everything aside and accompanied her husband to their bedroom, where they got down on their knees and began to thank God for their "miracle."

The following day Brother Palmer went to the owner of the property and made arrangements to purchase it.

Across the bridge on the other side of the property was a building that was used as a private school. Immediately they decided to start having services with the children and another single woman, Daisy Jones, whom they discovered had the Holy Ghost and was eager to find a place to worship. They continued worshiping there for the next few years, waiting on the next move of God.

On April 30, 1972, the groundbreaking ceremony was held. The Lord allowed Molly and her husband to give birth to Kings Chapel United Pentecostal Church, which has grown to produce many ministers and over thirty-six churches internationally.

Molly served in every area of church building with her husband, Pastor A. T. Palmer, who later became the superintendent of the Western District. He continued working with the Jamaica Mutual Insurance Company and was again offered another promotion—this time to return to the Kingston head office as president of the company. After much prayer and counseling from the national and international superintendents, Brother Palmer accepted the position. This took him into the company of all government leaders. Pastor Palmer commuted by air each week to the Kingston office, and returned to the Montego Bay church on weekends. Molly was kept busy with the administration of the church.

She was assistant pastor for approximately twenty-two years until the passing of her husband. Then she became the pastor and continued as pastor for eight years. She was the first Western District missions director and served in that position for twenty years. She was the first president of the Western Campus of Caribbean Bible Institute, and she also taught at youth camps.

The night before her husband died, Friday, February 11, 1989, she got up at approximately 2 A.M. to find her two daughters and their husbands with her husband in their bedroom. They informed her that some time before she had suffered a seizure and was unconscious to the point where her children and the doctor had to be called to the home.

At that time the cause of her illness could not be diagnosed, so her husband was told to take her to the hospital for some examinations and tests. This he did and then left her there so he could attend the funeral of one of his co-workers. The tests were done, but the doctors were puzzled as everything seemed normal.

Sometime in the evening, after relating to her the results of her condition, the doctors informed her of her husband's sudden death. Lying there on her back, she asked, "What do you mean?" Of course, this was out of shock, since she could not believe that he, being well enough to take her to the hospital, went back home and died. When she became more fully aware of the situation, she worshiped and resigned in her mind that "God knows best."

Their son-in-law, who had taken her husband to another hospital, reported that on their way to the hospital, Brother Palmer told him, "Everything will soon be all right."

She has continued to live believing that statement.

"Molly" (Imorette Rebecca) Palmer

Thirteen years have passed, and she still wonders why her life was spared and his taken. But it has been a time of varying kinds of experiences that have drawn and are still drawing her closer to the Lord, enabling her to see why she should love her Lord and serve Him more earnestly. The anointing and the presence of the Lord are still rich in her life even as she reveals her story.

by Imorette Rebecca Palmer and
Susan Palmer Gallimore (daughter)

The Palmers, pastors of Kings Chapel UPCI;
Montego Bay, Jamaica

CHAPTER Sixteen

Mary Alice Floyd Paslay

Reverend Mrs. Mary Alice Paslay was born Mary Alice Floyd on March 20, 1920, to Claude and Nancy Floyd in Muncie, Indiana. She had one sibling, her older brother, Robert Leon Floyd. Home to her in Muncie was a one-room housing unit referred to as a flat. The bathroom was more like a closet, housing only a toilet—no sink or tub. A pan was used for bathing. Six people were crammed into this one flat: Mary Alice, her parents, her brother, her grandmother, and her step-grandfather.

Nancy Floyd was a factory worker. Claude Floyd worked as a skilled laborer. However, he squandered the money he earned to support his drinking habit, leaving very little for his family to exist on. Mary Alice collected milk bottles to have money to go to the movie house, the only escape she enjoyed from the harsh reality in which she lived. She and her mother stood in line for free milk and nickel-per-loaf bread. Amidst all this, she recalled not realizing that they were poor.

Not only was Mary Alice poor, but she was also very

217

lonely while growing up. Robert Leon showed no interest in his little sister. Sadly, her father also lacked interest in having any meaningful relationship with his family. She was void of companionship in those sensitive days of childhood. As she grew older, her eyes began to open to the poverty in which she lived. She was suddenly embarrassed about her home, and she would have friends leave her at a certain point. When they were out of sight, she would walk the rest of the distance home.

The Floyd family did not attend church; however, Mrs. Floyd consistently sent young Mary Alice to a Church of God Sunday school. In 1932 a tent revival with R. O. Bear and his guitar came to town only a couple of blocks from their home in Muncie. Finally, at the age of thirteen, a flicker of hope entered into the life of Mary Alice Floyd when her mother decided to attend this apostolic tent revival.

These two lives were forever changed as they both received the Holy Ghost and were baptized in Jesus' name. The tent revival grew into a church constructed of blocks. Therefore, they referred to it as the "block church" on Delhoit Avenue.

Mary Alice and her mother walked to church regardless of the weather. Occasionally some of the saints would take them home. Nancy Floyd instructed her daughter how to sacrifice and fight for anything worthwhile. Simply attending church presented a challenge for the two of them. Mr. Floyd created an obstacle with his constant threats that he would cut their hair if they continued to go to church. The road was not easy, but they were determined. Mary Alice said that her mother possessed iron in her soul like that of Joseph.

Eventually the church that they attended split due to some questionable actions in the leadership. Disappointed but not disheartened, the Floyd women were among those who felt it necessary to leave. Mary Alice, who was already preaching at age fifteen, was asked to pastor the group.

Displaying wisdom in her youth, she declined, understanding that it takes more than good preaching to pastor a church. T. J. Miller became the pastor. The other men whom Mary Alice and her mother had prayed through to the Holy Ghost began a daughter work from this church.

While the Holy Ghost incited joy in her soul and meaning in her life, Mary Alice was faced with new social challenges as she entered high school. She felt once again the loneliness so familiar in her early childhood. Committed to answering the call of God on her life, she continued to live the challenge.

Mary Alice was a powerful preacher from the start. Early on she was asked to preach at her home church both in the "block" church before the split and in the new church that she attended. Invitations were frequently open for her to preach at youth rallies as well.

Youth rallies were a great opportunity for young, aspiring preachers. Many of them were given invitations to preach at the same youth rally. The schedule had to accommodate as many as were able to come. Come they did, whatever way they could. Mary Alice said she rode in a truck. She remembered there being no microphones and no music, only testimonies and preaching. She called that her Bible school.

Mary Alice's preaching was so anointed that her name was becoming known among the churches. She received an invitation from Ace Summers to preach a revival. "I didn't know how to preach a revival. I was nineteen and I had never been away from home," Sister Paslay later said. She preached in the small, country churches; then God began to enlarge her territory. "Now instead of going to all the little country churches, it was just bang—I was preaching in all the big churches, some of the biggest churches in that part of the country—Mt. Vernon and Herrin, Illinois, and St. Louis. It was God. It wasn't me," Sister Paslay stated.

When asked what it was like to be a female preacher, Sister Paslay said her call from God was very real. She believed that it was the women's rights movement that ruined God-given opportunities for women. Before the movement, women were more confidently able to answer the call of God on their lives, she believed. After the movement, women were more likely to be hindered by fear of the connotation their call to preach might have. It is a reminder to us of what a unique and brave woman of God she was.

Mary Alice's favorite message to preach was entitled "The Bride of Christ." In the message she spoke about the fitting of the bridal gown. She preached that God doesn't change the bridal gown to fit us but rather changes us to fit the gown.

After graduating from high school, Mary Alice began working in a dime store. She earned enough money to buy an accordion. "I bought an accordion and I did take one lesson, but I didn't really play the thing in public until I was married. The first time I played was in a little country church where we held our first revival together. I was going to play for them, and I was so embarrassed that I played with only one finger," she laughingly recalled.

The paths of Mary Alice Floyd and Norman R. Paslay crossed at the 1941 General Conference. A mutual friend introduced them, and initial impressions were not love at first sight. She concluded that he was not overly friendly. So for the time being, that was that.

Months later, Pastor J. H. Reeter of Vandalia, Illinois—Brother Paslay's home church—invited the widely known evangelist, Mary Alice Floyd, to preach a revival. She accepted and was at first perplexed by the young Norman R. Paslay, whom she had recently met. Every night he arrived early to be sure to get a front row seat in her direct view. She was not sure of his intent; actually, she thought he might be trying to intimidate her. Though a bit distracted, her preaching was unfeigned, and she was so powerfully anointed that members of the Methodist church across the street came to hear her as soon as their service was dismissed.

Later in the revival, she learned that the young gentleman on the front row whom she had judged unfriendly was an admirer. They were introduced for the second time, and from then love began to grow. After the revival, she returned home to Muncie and the two began correspondence. The Reverend Norman R. Paslay and Reverend Mary Alice Floyd were married only months later on October 29, 1942. They shared a double wedding with Brother Paslay's high school friend who had invited him to church for the first time.

The newlywed Brother and Sister Paslay accepted the pastorate of a church in Farina, Illinois. It was a small, coal-mining town with no streetlights. One night after service, they came home to find, much to their surprise, a woman "madder than a wet hen" sitting on their bed. At church they had been singing, and during the song, Sister Paslay addressed those that didn't love their neighbor. She said, "If you love your neighbor, say 'amen.'" The lady thought Sister Pasley was talking about her. "I told her that I didn't mean her. I was horrified." The woman had come to their home afterward wanting to know who had told them about her. Brother and Sister Paslay assured her that no one had told them anything.

Brother and Sister Paslay owned their first car while pastoring in Farina. It was a Ford with a rumble seat. They named it Amy Ruth. They bought it to be able to pick up people for church.

They had pastored for approximately one year when they felt the call to the evangelistic field. During their first revival together, an offering was collected for one dollar. On the road home, Brother Paslay, mistaking the dollar for a piece of paper, tossed it out the window. Receiving an offering was not commonplace in those days. Sister Paslay remembered an offering being taken one night a week. "Maybe they'd give it to you and maybe they wouldn't. We definitely were not in it for the money," she recalled.

Sister Paslay said that those twelve years of evangelism were rewarding, although to hear some of their tales, it is hard to imagine having such an attitude. "Some places we went hungry. Some places we had to sneak food into our room to be able to eat without offending the host. One place in particular we were staying in an upstairs room. It was the dead of winter, and they kept the door shut so we got no heat," she said. Brother Paslay would sit on her clothes to warm them for her. Sometimes not even their expenses were paid.

One preacher was so embarrassed about their car that he suggested they have glass put in where oilcloth hung. "We named the car after Matthew the tax collector because it cost so much," Sister Paslay related. They had learned from an older preacher, though, never to talk about how they had been treated to their next host. Sister Paslay said they were well advised, for if they had complained, word would have spread and they would no longer be invited anywhere. No doubt because of their experiences, Brother and Sister Paslay were two of the most generous hosts to young preachers, going above and beyond any obligation.

During their twelve years of evangelism, they ministered not only to thousands of adults, but they also touched the hearts of children and young people everywhere they ministered. Their powerful children's ministry began with "Oscar," Sister Paslay's first puppet, which she purchased for thirty-nine cents. Sister Paslay also ministered to children with her vivid Scene-o-Felt illustrations. They ministered just as earnestly to children as to adults in many camps and revival services. Later they would minister especially to children during chapel services at their Christian academy.

Sister Paslay really knew how to impart conviction into the hearts of children. With her mask called "two faced," she graphically illustrated how sin works in our lives. One side of her mask was glamorously beautiful, showing how sin makes itself appealing, and the other side was grotesque, demonstrating how sin deceives and only shows its good side. The message was powerful.

Brother and Sister Paslay also ministered together in music. With her accordion and his stand-up bass, they formed a harmonious duet. Their music was a delight to anyone within earshot. Later they recorded several albums with many of their friends and fellow workers in the ministry. They recorded their first album at an RCA recording studio in Cincinnati with "The Gospel Melodies," the first Pentecostal record company. The recording cost them two hundred dollars. Among the albums, they recorded what would become their lifelong theme: "We Are a Happy People."

Called to Cincinnati in 1953, the Paslays left the evangelistic field. Brother Paslay became the assistant pastor, and they served faithfully. During one service they announced their "latest release": Norman R. Paslay II born on March 26, 1957. Tearfully, Sister Paslay recalled having prayed for a son who would do more for the kingdom of God than they ever could.

Suddenly, a storm of vicious accusation came against Brother Paslay, a storm so strong few would have weathered it, but the Paslays did. Their loyalty and integrity were devastatingly brought into question. Sister Paslay recounted her hurt being so deep for her husband. She knew how pure his motives were. She knew what kind of man he was. "I was the first girl he ever kissed. He didn't even know how to pucker," she said. Sister Paslay was deeply wounded by the falsehood brought against her husband.

The Paslays were tried before the General Board in St. Louis for the accusations brought against them. It was an especially difficult time for both of them. They had signed the original merger that began the United Pentecostal Church International. They were found innocent of all charges and remained in fellowship with the UPCI. Even their accusers were apologetic for their accusations. Through this storm, they were victorious.

During this test of the Paslays' faith, God did not release them from their call to Cincinnati. Nor did they abandon their call, which would have been the easy route. Instead, Brother and Sister Paslay founded Calvary Pentecostal Church on December 8, 1968. Even today a stone engraved "Ezel" from the story of David in I Samuel stands as a reminder of the trial and triumph through which the church was born. The ministry of Brother and Sister Paslay was not a self-serving career but a lifelong desire to "The Will of God At Any Cost" as states the sign still hanging on the wall at Calvary Church. Though simple in its attraction, this motto is a reminder that we are called to a cause greater than ourselves.

While exasperated by the battles fought and won during this trying time, Brother and Sister Paslay never ran out of time to spend with their son. He, too, was affected by the trials he watched his parents endure. And while there was sadness, the Paslays were careful not to forget their family.

The Paslay trio lived on Pell Street in what was called Northside in Cincinnati. Sighs of comic relief are sweet humming melodies as the stories of Pell Street are revisited. One warm summer day, Sister Paslay hung the freshly-washed laundry out to dry. However, when the clothesline was emptied and the clothes were brought into the house, something unusual happened. A bat came flying out of a pocket of one of Brother Paslay's shirts. The three of them, stunned by the intrusion, couldn't think quickly enough about what to do. Sister Paslay turned to Brother Paslay and realized that she and young

Norman had been abandoned to fend for themselves. Brother Paslay had taken shelter beneath the bedroom sheets.

Life on Pell Street offered a great opportunity for the Paslays to instill great faith into their son. A hole in the floor from a plumbing problem indicated that many repairs were needed. Brother Paslay, understanding the need but never one to panic, went to his young son and told him of the situation. "There is a hole. We have no money. Would you help me pray?" Pray they did, and the answer came. A check arrived in the mail from someone impressed by the Lord to give the exact amount of money to fill the need.

In the physical, Brother and Sister Paslay had only one son. In the spiritual, they fostered many. Brother Paslay birthed Jonathan Ministries on March 3, 1974. Today it continues to be a vital asset in the church in Cincinnati as well as across the nation, a ministry to help upcoming ministers and their families financially with expenses for things like tires or a much needed suit or to replace a worn-out pair of shoes—just to meet a need.

This was Brother Paslay's burden; but as in everything else, Sister Paslay provided great support and was a complement to him.

The Paslays invited Pastor Rick Flowers into town. He was one of their Jonathans. Sister Paslay jumped right in to support her husband's ministry. In a way that only she could, she let Brother Flowers know that he dressed like an old man and Jonathan Ministries would definitely have to make a way to provide him with some more clothes.

Not left unscathed by years of hardship as a child, a young woman preacher, a wife, and a mother, Sister

Paslay allowed the Lord to use her as He willed. Her mother was always very special to her, so after her mother's death, she wrote an article for the *Ohio News* entitled "Color Me Beautiful." Along with the article was a painting by Brother Lee Stoneking illustrating the three stages of the butterfly. The butterfly would become a symbol that represents the life and ministry of a one-of-a-kind, great lady.

Like the butterfly, the life of Reverend Mrs. Mary Alice Paslay was a portrait entitled "Color Me Beautiful" created by the Master's artistic hand. The colorful brush strokes of her life represented her many ministries. She invested her life and prayers into people of all ages with an unwavering passion. Through the butterfly's story, Sister Paslay ministered to thousands of lives, and God gave us a grand illustration in her. Her godly charisma, exceptional wisdom, and sparkling good humor shall always be missed but never forgotten.

Her journey to live her message of change under God in "Color Me Beautiful" was completed on April 7, 1999, when she left sickness and pain to be in paradise with her Lord. The church and family she gave her life for continue to grow in impact and power as they follow the vision and path her life put before them.

by Norman R. Paslay II (son)

*Mary Alice with
mother and
brother*

*Childhood picture of
Mary Alice Floyd
(Paslay)*

Mary Alice as a teenager

Mary Alice Floyd Paslay

*Evangelist Mary Alice
Floyd*

*Brother
and Sister
Paslay*

229

Campmeeting evangelis
Brother and Sister Paslo

Sister Paslay

Musician, Mary
Alice Paslay

CHAPTER Seventeen

Carmen Quiles

It was the year 1963. I was in New York City, waiting for orders to be moved to another base with my Navy husband. He had told me that we might be going to California.

As I prayed, I asked the Lord to help me find a good Pentecostal church close enough that I could walk because I didn't have a car and couldn't drive.

I had received the Holy Ghost but didn't know anything about water baptism in Jesus' name. As I prayed, the Lord spoke to me and said, "From the window of your house, you will see the church where you will serve Me." I rejoiced as I claimed that promise.

Orders came to move to Pensacola, Florida. As soon as I got to the apartment at the Navy station, I looked out the window to see if there was a church building nearby. Nowhere could I see one.

I asked my next-door neighbor if there was a church close by. She told me that there was not one. Well, I knew within my heart that the Lord had spoken to me, so I was comforted and felt at ease. I started going to the base chapel until I could find a Pentecostal church, for I needed to take my children to Sunday school.

One day as I was praying, I was impressed to look through the list of churches in the yellow pages of the telephone book. There were four Pentecostal churches listed, but I wanted the one closest to me. So I closed my eyes and pointed to one. It was the East Gasden United Pentecostal Church.

I wrote a letter to the pastor at the address in the book. A week later there was a knock at my door; when I opened it, there stood two men. One of them had the letter I had written in his hand. He asked, "Did you write this letter?"

I said, "Yes," and they introduced themselves as Pastor A. D. Morris and Brother Charles Mimms.

I invited them to come in and we talked for a while. Pastor Morris told me that the church was seven miles away but that he would come and get my family and me for Sunday school. He even said that we could drive his car home in order for my husband to bring us back for the night service. We didn't have a car, and this was the way he had of getting us back.

We started attending regularly, going on Sunday morning when he came to pick us up, tempting the children with doughnuts that he would pick up on the way. After Sunday school, he would leave the car with my husband to drive home and return for the night service.

My children, Lourdes, Peter, and Vicky, loved him. It was a repeat each Sunday. However, on Wednesday night when he brought us home, he kept his car.

There was just one thing that I pondered in my heart.

There was so much teaching on Wednesday night about one God. Baptism in Jesus' name was new and strange to me. I wrote to my former pastor in Puerto Rico about what I was hearing. He quickly wrote back for me to "get out of that church. They are the Jesus Name people and teach a false doctrine."

I did not know what to do because in the meanwhile I was seeing people receiving the Holy Ghost and being baptized, not in the titles but in the name of Jesus. How they rejoiced when they came out of the water!

How confused and surprised I was. I wondered how this could be false doctrine. For a while I continued going since Brother Morris kept coming for us. But I finally made up my mind that I would let the pastor know that we wouldn't be back anymore.

So one Wednesday night, when Brother Morris brought us home, he parked the car. As I was getting out, I opened my mouth to speak but that was as far as I got because he said, "Oh, Sister, here. Take these scriptures with you. Read them, study them, and call me when you are ready to be baptized."

I was surprised. How did he know that I was not planning to come back? While studying the Scripture passages, my eyes filled with tears so that at times the pages of my Bible would become wet with my tears. I truly was receiving the revelation of water baptism in the precious name of Jesus but yet could not agree to let myself be baptized.

One day while reading in Acts 19, I found that some disciples had been rebaptized in the name of Jesus. I called Brother Morris and told him that I was ready to be baptized in Jesus' name. That night he baptized my husband, children, and me in the name of Jesus, the name above all names.

I asked Pastor Morris, "Why don't we have somebody in Puerto Rico preaching this message?" He answered that he did not know but that he was going to the General Conference in Tennessee and would find out.

He went to that conference and to his surprise, going into an elevator with him was Brother Vouga, the director of foreign missions, and a couple whom he introduced as Brother and Sister Glen Smith, newly appointed missionaries going to live in Puerto Rico! Brother Morris introduced himself as the pastor of the United Pentecostal Church in Pensacola and stated that he had a couple in his church from Puerto Rico, Sister Carmen and her husband Julio and three children. He asked if they would come and preach for him.

Brother Smith quickly put scheduled revivals on hold. This started a wonderful friendship with the Smiths. My husband allowed me to go to Puerto Rico even though I was expecting my youngest child, a son we named Josué.

The Smiths arrived by freighter on February 25, 1964, and with permission from my husband, I went in March to help them and was their interpreter. I also witnessed to my mother and saw her baptized in Jesus' name.

After two months I returned to Pensacola for the birth of my healthy baby boy. Shortly after that, my husband was transferred to Jacksonville, Florida. We moved to a rented house. As soon as we moved I looked out the windows, trying everywhere to find the church building God had promised me, for He had said, "From the window of your house, you will see the church." There was not a church to view from my window, so we visited Brother Childres's church in Jacksonville.

It was time to be transferred again, but this time we were moving to Roosevelt Roads, the U.S. Navy base in Puerto Rico! Was I happy! Yes, how I longed to be there to proclaim the message of baptism in Jesus' name and work with the Smiths.

While living in a rented house in Ceiba, near the Navy base, my father-in-law retired from his job working at *The New York Times* and wanted to give some money so that we could purchase some property and build a house.

We found an acre of land in Ceiba, near the Navy base at Roosevelt Roads, and called Brother and Sister Smith to come, see the land, pray, and dedicate it. When he finished praying he said, "You have enough land for not only your house but also a church." We built a small wooden house and moved into it. Later when they again visited us, he asked, "Where do you want to put the church?" I answered with just a few words as my husband smiled and nodded in agreement, "Right over there."

When we wrote up the deed giving the piece of land to the church, Brother Smith began to build right away. I forgot what the Lord had promised me.

As the walls of the church building were being built, one day Sister Smith was in my house doing some cooking with me for the workers of the church building. All at once I started crying and praising God at the same time as I looked out my kitchen window. I had not yet told her about the promise God had given me. When she asked me what was happening, I told her and we had a rejoicing time together.

The church dedication was March 7, 1970. That night

Brother Smith called me aside and told me that he wanted to leave me in charge of the church services. I opened my mouth to say, "No, Brother Smith, please don't ask that of me." But he said for me to start having prayer meetings and children's church and that he would come and do some teaching. In the beginning it was just my family. But other people began to come, and then more people started visiting. It was a growing church that I pastored until 1975. I could see the church from the kitchen window of my small wooden house. Later we built a larger house on the property, a short walk from the church.

I had quit school in 1945 when my father died and my mother was left with seven children. I started back to school in March 1970. Two months after that, I passed the tests and was promoted to the ninth grade. I finished high school and was asked to teach English in the third grade at a school near my home. After finishing high school, I went on to the university to qualify to be a teacher. I had a desire to do more for the Lord.

The International Bible Institute of the Caribbean in Puerto Rico began with its opening night on December 19, 1970, with classes during the winter to spring months of 1971. The teachers invited by Brother Smith, the president, were Brothers Hulan Myers, F. V. Shoemake, Frank Munsey, Paul Froese, and Fred Foster. The classes were held in the new two-story church building, dedicated in 1966, in Santurce. How we treasured these valuable lessons.

Brother Smith asked me to be the interpreter for all the classes taught by our American brethren. I gladly consented and came by public car forty-five miles each way from Ceiba to Rio Piedras every class day, five days a week. At that time there was no Spanish literature for the Bible school and only a few books in English. As I interpreted on the blackboard in Spanish, the students copied the notes into their notebooks. These notes became their first study books.

We had many pastors visiting the island to preach conferences and youth camps. I was translator for all the messages.

I remember Brother Fred Kinzie preaching about the "Salmon Run." I had never heard of the amazing feats of the salmon, leaping through rapids and up waterfalls. All I knew about the word salmon was the slang word used as street language. So I was stopped "cold" to look at Brother Kinzie and ask, "What is that?" He took time to explain and continued with his message.

Another minister came and said we were going to have a "ball" in this place. Again I had to stop for I didn't know how to tell our people we were going to have a "ball." I'll never forget Brother Robert Henson preaching with the theme "Yo no sé," translated, "I don't know." It has been wonderful meeting so many of God's people and serving Him all these years.

Upon my resignation of the church in Ceiba in 1975, Brother Joaquin Morale, who is now the national superintendent, and his wife became pastor and have enlarged the church with a second floor. I felt led to start a church in Fajardo where we had only a small group of people.

God had spoken to me, and I approached Brother Smith after finding some vacant land. He said, "Sister Carmen, you know the bank won't lend money without a building on it." However, I knew the wife of the president of the bank. He had confidence in me and we got the loan.

Brother Smith first built a small wooden church building on the two large lots. My oldest daughter had her wedding there.

As the church membership grew, again God spoke to me and gave me a vision of a larger building. I also considered a day school.

We went to an architect. However, upon our return to see the drawings we knew that the layout that he had drawn was far beyond our expectations and told him so. Then he smiled and said, "The Lord directed me in doing this. Now He will direct you to build for His glory." The drawing called for a two-story building: the first floor for schoolrooms and the top story for the worship services.

Pastor C. D. Thornton, of Lake Charles, came with a group from his church to preach the conference in the Dominican Republic. Before returning to the States, he gave several thousand dollars on the building in Fajardo to be built; later he returned for the dedication services.

Brother Smith and brethren of the district came and worked mixing cement by hand with a shovel all day long in the hot tropical climate. Brother Smith at sixty years of age stood on a ladder, and somebody would swing the bucket of cement up to him. It was hard work, but God helped them and a beautiful building was completed, a lighthouse to the community of Fajardo. Since I retired from pastoring, my nephew, Brother Michack Lespier, has become pastor, and the church is blessed by his ministry.

I also had the privilege of serving as the president of the Ladies Auxiliary of Puerto Rico for twenty-five years. During these years, activities and projects were not only to promote the work in Puerto Rico but the needs in the other islands in order to see the work of God move forward.

Having been retired from pastoring now for many years, I still stay involved in teaching Bible school classes and ministering in the district and also speaking in ladies' Spanish seminars in the States. I was privileged to attend the ladies' seminar in the Dominican Republic on October 2002. I have been asked to be the interpreter for Sister Gwyn Oakes, the international president of the Ladies Ministries. I'm looking forward to being with her as well as Brother and Sister Steve Shirley, the missionary superintendent, for another great conference.

I am grateful for the support that my husband continues to give me in all the situations in which God has allowed me to be involved.

The Lord's promise that He gave me, of seeing a church through the window of my home, has taught me that I can truly trust Him for whatever life may bring; for whatever He promises, He will do.

"Sister Carmen is a Christian lady who had the courage to change and overcome obstacles and difficulties in her life. First, she determined to put God first and then seek a better education in order to prepare herself for whatever work God had in store for her. I was thrilled when Sister Mary Wallace asked her to write her story, for it is one that deserves to be told. (To tell all, many more pages would have to be written.) Truly she has and continues to be a willing vessel unto the Lord."

–Rachel Smith (Retired Missionary Wife)

by Carmen Quiles

*Brother and Sister Carmen Quiles at celebration
of 50th wedding anniversary, 1999*

CHAPTER Eighteen

Agnes Rich

Five-year-old Agnes Caughron whimpered against the hot, smothering darkness of a Texas summer night as the fiery pain in her legs gnawed at her sleep and burst through it. In agony, she rubbed her legs against the sheets, trying to ease their intolerable burning and itching. One thin little leg, in its jerking, kicked her younger sister, Billie, curled on the mattress beside her.

"Agnes, stop," Billie mumbled as she rolled away from Agnes back into sleep.

But Agnes couldn't stop. She sat up in bed, pulling her knees under her chin as she stroked her impetigo-covered legs.

"Don't scratch your legs, Agnes," her mother had cautioned her time and time again. "That will only make the itching worse."

So Agnes, trying to obey, sat hunched in the thin moonlight, rubbing her hands lightly across the scabs as tears scalded her cheeks. Up and down, from ankle to knee and back again, her fingers vainly strove to chase the hurt away. The touch only intensified the agonizing pain. She arched her fingers and clawed at her legs, giving in to the impulse to find relief at any cost. Tears dripped off her chin onto her knees as she struggled to muffle her sobs.

Mother mustn't hear me and wake up, she thought. *Mother is tired.*

But Mother did hear. Agnes heard her mother's light step and smelled the perfume of her mother's nearness. Then her dear mother's arms encircled her and a soft, cool cheek was laid against her wet, feverish one as slender arms scooped her from the bed and carried her into the kitchen.

"It hurts," Agnes wailed.

"I know, honey," Johnny Caughron sympathized as she put Agnes on a chair. Turning, she swiftly dipped water into a bowl and then wrung out clean rags and wrapped them around the flaming legs.

Agnes's breath shuddered in her chest and her sobs became hiccups. The cool wetness helped her legs a little. Her mother's loving ministrations and softly murmured prayers helped more.

"Better?" Mother smoothed Agnes's sweat-drenched hair from her forehead. Agnes nodded. A few minutes later when the pain eased to a toleration point, Agnes crept back to bed and fell asleep.

The next night the scene was repeated. And the next.

"Will my legs ever be better, Mom?" Agnes asked one day as Johnny sat rocking the baby. The little girl sat Indian style, idly picking at the crustiest scab. There wasn't a square inch of healthy skin anywhere on her legs; what wasn't scabbed over oozed a thin, sticky liquid from raw sores. The impetigo had defied all of Johnny's homemade potions and scorned the well-meant suggestions of other mothers in the neighborhood.

The rocking chair creaked as her mother's toe kept it in motion. Tap, squeak. Tap, squeak. Agnes, looking up, saw her mother staring at her over the baby's shoulder.

"Will they, Mom?"

Agnes wiggled under her mother's gaze. There was something in her mother's face she'd never seen before, and although it didn't frighten her, it sent little squiggles up and down her spine.

"Yes, Agnes, I believe they will," Mother said slowly. She stopped rocking and carried the sleeping baby to bed. Agnes ran out to play.

That night as Agnes skipped ahead of her mother and father while the family walked to revival services at the small church about four blocks from the house, the little girl overheard snatches of her parents' conversation.

"The Scriptures say to anoint with oil . . ."

". . . been praying for the sick . . ."

". . . was healed of . . ."

". . . Agnes's legs . . ."

Still, she was surprised when sometime during the service her mother motioned to her. "Agnes," Mother whispered, "Pastor Davis is getting ready to pray for the sick. Your dad and I are going to take you up and have the pastor anoint you with oil and pray for you. Jesus can heal your legs."

Tucking one hand into her mother's and the other into her dad's, Agnes walked between them to the front of the church. She watched the pastor tip a small bottle of oil against his finger. As his oil-laden finger touched her forehead, she closed her eyes and wrinkled her nose against its smell. In her ears she could hear her parents' voices mixing with her pastor's. Behind her, the prayers of the saints swelled into the corners of the sanctuary.

Back in her seat, Agnes surveyed her legs. They looked the same: yellowish-brown scabs, red sores shiny with seepage. And they still burned and itched.

But Agnes slept all through the night. When she woke up, something scratched her legs. The bed was full of pokey things that felt like dried bread crumbs. Agnes yanked the sheet back, took one look at her legs, and started yelling.

"My legs! Jesus healed my legs! Mom, come see!"

Agnes hopped from the bed, jumping up and down on beautiful, pink-skinned legs. No raw sores scored their velvety normalcy. No scars marred the smooth, new skin.

"Look, Mom!" Agnes said when Johnny came running. "My legs are brand-new!" She stuck out a leg for her mother to see. Then she pointed to the bed.

Dried bread crumbs? No, just scabs—handfuls of them pushed off a child's legs by newly formed skin—mutely testifying to the healing power of Jesus Christ.

From that time on with all her heart, Agnes Ruth Caughron wanted to serve the Lord.

After the Lord healed her legs, she began going to the altar "just like all the grown-ups." There she repented of her sins and soon afterward begged her parents to let her be baptized.

"Agnes, I think you're too young," her father said. E. W. himself had known the Lord for less than a year and was somewhat startled by the idea of a child so young feeling her need for God.

"Please," Agnes begged. "The Bible says I have to be baptized in Jesus' name."

"Honey, you're only five years old," Mother reminded her.

"We'll talk to the pastor about it," E. W. finally agreed. "But Agnes, if he thinks you should wait awhile, then you'll have to wait."

To Agnes's delight, however, Pastor A. S. Davis advised her parents to consent to her being baptized. "I've been watching Agnes," he told them, "and I believe God really is dealing with her."

So a few weeks before her sixth birthday, Agnes, dressed in a little white dress she loved to wear, was baptized in Jesus' name for the remission of her sins.

Shortly afterward, God called E. W. and Johnny into the ministry. Life in the dust-bowl years of the Great Depression was difficult, and especially so for young evangelists with three small children. Often even food was scarce, and what little there was provided monotonous fare.

During a revival, the local pastor usually arranged for the saints to bring food to the Caughrons. In a revival in Singer, Louisiana, however, everyone's garden had produced an abundance of potatoes, so that is what everyone brought. One man who attended the revival but wasn't yet in the church gave them a leg of mutton. But Johnny had no salt with which to season the food. Offerings often consisted of coins—small ones at that—and those had to be kept for needs more urgent than salt.

For several days, Agnes ate the unsalted mutton and swallowed her portion of unseasoned potatoes. The little girl hungered for a change in her diet. More than anything else, she yearned for a slice of bread and jelly—mayhaw jelly, her favorite.

Sitting in a daub of shade on the front porch of the little house in which they were living, Agnes felt her stomach growl.

"Mom, what are we having for supper?" Agnes asked her mother, who was sitting in the porch swing.

"Potatoes and mutton," her mother replied.

Agnes felt her stomach heave. Hungry as she was, she thought that if she had to eat one more bite of potatoes and mutton she'd throw up!

Maybe Mother will pray and God will send us something else to eat, she thought. She had great faith in Mother's prayers, for not only had she seen many of those prayers wonderfully answered, but she still remembered the impetigo-ridden legs.

She inspected those legs now. One of the worst, most tormenting sores had been right there. Agnes prodded the smooth, sun-browned skin and watched the whitened finger mark resolve itself as she lifted her finger away. Two bruises—one new purple and the other old green—and a healthy, play-acquired layer of Texas dust mottled her legs, but there was no trace of the impetigo.

If God can make the impetigo go away, He should be able to send me some bread and jelly, she reasoned. *Maybe Mother will pray for bread and jelly if I ask her to.* Just thinking of a slice of thick bread, brown crusted and meltingly soft in its white middle, layered with bright red mayhaw jelly, brought a flood of saliva to her mouth.

But it wouldn't be right to ask Mother to pray, Agnes thought. *After all, Mother has enough to do, cooking and keeping house and preaching and praying. Maybe Dad . . . no, bread and jelly were a woman's business.* Besides, Mom and Dad hadn't said anything about wanting bread and jelly. It was her want, not theirs.

Agnes picked at a splinter, trying to make up her mind. Since she was the one wanting the bread and jelly, shouldn't she be the one to pray for it? But what if God didn't like being bothered by a little girl's prayers for bread and jelly? Would He be mad at her for asking? She scrambled to her feet and trotted to the other end of the porch.

"Mom, do you think the Lord would mind if I prayed and asked Him for some jelly and bread?"

The porch swing stopped creaking as her dad planted both feet on the floor. "Agnes, you're tired of mutton and potatoes, aren't you?" he asked.

Agnes nodded. "But would Jesus think I'm selfish and unthankful for the mutton if I asked Him for bread and jelly?"

The little girl didn't understand the look that passed between her parents, but she understood her mother's reply.

"Honey, Jesus loves you," Johnny said. "If you want bread and jelly that much, it's all right to pray and ask Him for it."

Agnes scampered off. She knew the perfect prayer place, separate and private. Running to the old Model T Ford parked in the yard, she climbed into the back seat and yanked the door closed behind her. Hanging over the back of the seat, she rolled up the front windows. Then she dropped to her knees between the seats. Dust rose in twin puffs where her elbows pressed craters into the upholstery. It tickled her nose and tiny pebbles on the floor ground into her knees, but she ignored those inconsequential things as she asked the Lord to send her some bread and jelly.

Leaving the car, she resumed her spot on the porch. Even Billie, begging her to come play tag, could not budge her from her vigil.

"Agnes, you are so still," her father said. "What are you doing?"

"I'm waiting for my bread and jelly," Agnes answered. She risked being rude by not turning around, but she had to watch the street. She might miss her bread and jelly.

An old man shuffled past, his walking stick stirring up small dust eddies. Two women appeared, carrying baskets. Agnes jumped up, then sat down again. No, they were going to market. She could see a purse tucked under the arm of one of the ladies. In the side yard, Billie's squeals mingled with the yells of other kids as they played tag.

Agnes's square of shade angled across her lap as the sun dipped lower. Soon her mother would go into the house to fix supper. Agnes scooted back into the shade as a boy wobbled by on a rickety bicycle. Then Agnes spied a little girl about her own size down the street under the shadow of a big tree. The other little girl was heading straight toward Agnes, and Agnes saw she was carrying a brown paper sack. Agnes started to dash toward the gate, but she made herself smooth her hair and brush off her skirt as she'd seen her mother do when visitors came.

The small stranger pushed open the gate and walked right up to Agnes. "This is for you," she said bashfully, putting the sack into Agnes's outstretched hands.

"Thank you," Agnes said, remembering her manners.

With her left hand she could feel the square bottom of a Mason jar; with her right, she sensed something soft and resilient. As soon as the gate creaked closed behind her visitor, Agnes flung herself toward the house. Bounding up the steps, she raced across the porch.

Breathless with hurry, she laid the parcel in her father's lap. Reaching inside it, she pulled out the rarest of treats, a loaf of store-bought bread. Laying it reverently in her mother's lap, she gave it a loving pat and dived into the sack again.

Triumphantly she pulled out a quart of jelly and held it aloft. The sun pierced and lit its ruby depths. "My bread and jelly!" she cried. "The Lord sent me some bread and jelly!" She hugged the jar to her and twirled circles on the worn boards.

"Agnes, I do believe—I do believe that's mayhaw jelly," Mother said. "Your favorite."

Something tight and thick in her mother's voice snapped Agnes out of her jubilation and stopped her in mid-spin. She looked at her parents.

"Why are you crying?" she asked them.

In the years that followed, Agnes often clung to those two faith-building answers to prayer. Each had a special significance: The Lord's healing her legs was the first answered prayer she could remember; the Lord's sending her bread and jelly was the first answered prayer that she had prayed.

In 1932, her dad became the pastor of the church in Kimball Bend, Texas. And there, under his first pastorate, at a sawdust altar in an outdoor revival preached by her mother and Brother Powell Sojourner, Agnes received her personal Pentecost.

While she prayed, the seven-year-old child was caught away in a vision. God let her peek into heaven and see angels rejoicing over her salvation. When the vision faded and she "came back to earth," she thought she'd fallen asleep and dreamed about heaven. But as she tried to tell about her "dream" to the people gathered around her, she found she could not speak in her own language. Then she realized she had received the Holy Ghost. And although she did not know it at the time, this would be only her first experience with angels.

When Agnes was fifteen and Billie thirteen, the girls went to Mountain Top, Texas, to Bible school. While she attended the school, God called Agnes to preach, and she continued for many years faithfully serving God, enjoying a special "ministry of angels" in her last ten years of life. Perhaps there is a reason for that.

She evangelized throughout Texas, Louisiana, Mississippi, and Oklahoma. She founded two churches in Texas: one at Brownsville and another at Stephenville. Later, she followed her parents to Anchorage, Alaska, and pastored there while the Caughrons returned to Louisiana. When sickness prevented Brother Caughron's return to Alaska, Agnes stayed and supervised the construction of a building for the church her parents had begun. In 1962 God led her to pioneer the work in Grand Island, Nebraska. While there, Agnes endured the destructive effects of a flood, a devastating tornado, a daughter's serious health problems, and the deaths of her husband and her mother. She also broke her leg and ankle, suffered a severe financial loss, experienced a major heart attack and a light stroke, underwent emergency open-heart surgery and two surgeries for cancer—

all while she persevered through a four-year court case involving the Christian school sponsored by her church.

Throughout these trials, angels ministered to her repeatedly. They came to her home, to her church, to the courtroom, and to her hospital bed.

Of the last twenty-four months of her life, fourteen were spent in a hospital room. Agnes shared her angel experiences with many of the hospital staff over these long months. Just a few weeks prior to her death on September 14, 1993, Agnes, weak and sick from the complications of medication, told her sister, Thetus Tenney, that an angel had come again for just a few minutes. Anxiously, Thetus waited for her to tell about it, but all Agnes said was, "You can't know. It was just for me."

Angels had rejoiced when Agnes received the Holy Ghost. And no doubt they were still rejoicing over her life when it ended nearly sixty years later, for in all that time and during the half century of her ministry, Agnes Caughron Rich gave them many, many reasons to be jubilant.

by Dolly McElhaney and Thetus Tenney (sister)

Agnes Rich with three sisters and mom and dad. Agnes, Billie Lambert, Brother and Sister Caughron, Thetus Tenney, Becky Falls

Brother and Sister Rich

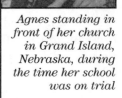

Agnes standing in front of her church in Grand Island, Nebraska, during the time her school was on trial

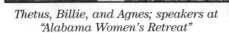

Thetus, Billie, and Agnes; speakers at "Alabama Women's Retreat"

Agnes Rich

CHAPTER Nineteen

Ruth Daniels Vouga

Ruth Daniels Vouga was born in South Bethlehem, Pennsylvania. Ruth's mother was a toe dancer for the Orpheum Circuit for five years. She could not continue her career and be a mother, so she paid Ruth's grandmother and aunts $600 per month to care for her.

At the age of four, Ruth's grandmother and aunts put her in the Methodist Episcopal Orphanage in Philadelphia, Pennsylvania. Later Ruth wondered, "Where's my mummy? What's my daddy's name?" She was told that her parents were dead. Life in the orphanage was very strict and rigid, sort of like being in the army.

Each year on Christmas Day, Ruth's aunts never had time to visit her. They came the day after.

One day when Ruth was about twelve years old, as she was sitting at the piano bench, one of the girls in the orphanage came running in and said, "Someone is in the hall wanting to see you!" Trembling, Ruth went to see who was in the hall.

The lady in the hall asked, "Do you know me, darling?"

"No, ma'am," Ruth answered.

"I've been looking for you all these years. I have searched and searched. Your grandmother and aunts would not tell me where you were. I want you to go with me now. Ruth, honey, I'm your mother."

What a shock for Ruth. She replied, "You can't be my mother. My mother is dead." Trembling and scared, Ruth kept repeating, "You're not my mother. I thought you were dead."

"Ruth, dear, I am your mother. Please come with me."

"I can't come now, Mother," the young girl answered.

Then Ruth's mother said, "I will be writing you. I am going to see what I can do to get you out of this place."

Time passed, and again Ruth lost track of her mother.

One of Ruth's aunts lived in an old folks' home next to the orphanage. One day this aunt came to the orphanage with a letter from Ruth's mother. She answered the letter, and her mother took the necessary steps to get Ruth out of the orphanage.

After the necessary steps were completed, Ruth was put on a train to live with her mother. She rode in the Pullman car with a matron on the train. In those days, matrons cared for young teenagers traveling alone.

Ruth had been given $10 to pay for her meals while on the train. In fear of train robbery, Ruth pinned the money to her slip. The train trip was a very frightening experience for the young girl. What would happen to her? Would she like her mother? What would her life be like?

Ruth knew nothing about train traveling. At supper time, she was in the washroom getting ready for supper. Finally she went up to a nice, motherly looking lady and told her that she was an orphan traveling alone. "Would you please go with me to the dining car?" she asked. The lady kindly agreed.

"Here I was, a scared young girl, on my way to Detroit, Michigan," Ruth later said. The kind lady took Ruth to the dining car and introduced her to her husband. The man then paid for Ruth's meal and helped look after her. The next morning the same caring couple took Ruth to breakfast and again paid for her meal.

When the train arrived in Detroit, Ruth was met by another stranger, her stepfather. He took her to her mother. Soon afterward, Ruth, her mother, and stepfather moved to Pontiac, Michigan.

Ruth soon found that her stepfather was quite a character. He was a traveling salesman, and a crooked one at that. With violent tendencies and evil ideas, the stepfather later threatened her very life. He told Ruth that he would get her, one way or another, even if he had to destroy her life with a gun. Fear gripped the young girl! *What can I do? What will happen?* she wondered. She was terrified.

Finally, Ruth told her mother about her stepfather's threats. Her mother, who was unsaved at this time, had a violent temper. Soon she divorced the stepfather. Later, due to his lifestyle, he ended up in prison.

Up to this point in time, Ruth had lived in constant fear. She was afraid of her mother's violent temper. When Ruth got a job and went to work, she would call home each evening to see what kind of mood her mother was in before going home.

One day Ruth's mother went to a department store to shop. While shopping, she was approached by a lady evangelist who was conducting meetings in town. The lady witnessed to her about her soul and insisted that she attend one of the meetings.

Out of curiosity, Ruth's mother went to the meeting. The pastor at the church was a very strong holiness preacher. Later Ruth said, "During that meeting my mother got under conviction and went to the altar.

"That night Mother prayed through, and God filled her with the Holy Ghost. What a miracle! When Mother got home, she was still speaking in other tongues. I couldn't believe that she was my mother, the change was so drastic. Before Mother was saved, she had a violent temper and a very proud spirit. Even the dog knew something was different.

"After a while, my mother got a call to take charge of an apartment house in Oakland, California. So we moved to Oakland. We were close to a good mission church pastored by Brother Harry Morse."

Ruth still was not saved at this time. Her mother was deeply concerned about her daughter's salvation. As for Ruth, the world had a very strong hold on her. She would say to her mother, "I'm too young to get saved. You had your good times. Now I am going to have mine."

Ruth later recalled, "One Saturday evening Mom went to the mission for church. It was 4 A.M. the next morning when she returned home. I was extremely worried about her. I walked the floor wondering what was keeping my mother so long. Did something happen to her? When the clock struck four the next morning and Mom returned home, I found that she had been in intercessory prayer for my soul. I did not let this bother me at all. I just said, 'Good night,' and went to bed.

"The next day, Sunday, reluctantly I went to church

with my mother. On the way down the stairs into the mission, Mother said, 'Daughter, you are going to be saved tonight.'

"I answered, 'Mother, I do not want salvation.' My mother did not answer me; she just smiled and kept on walking."

During the service the saints started to sing, "Where He Leads Me, I Will Follow." Something got hold of Ruth Daniels.

"I started weeping uncontrollably. One of the women in the church saw me and took me to the prayer room. In the prayer room, I got on my knees and repented with bitter tears. I wanted to lift my arm toward heaven, but I couldn't. You see, I had seven bracelets on one arm. Without anyone telling me that wearing bracelets was wrong, I reached over and pushed them off my arm and threw them on the floor. Up went my arms as I praised the Lord," Ruth recalled. God's Spirit and convicting power had gotten hold of Ruth Daniels. (From this point, the story is related by Sister Vouga.)

When I came to myself, I had received a good dose of the cleansing of the blood and salvation for repentance, but I did not receive the Holy Ghost that night. I was baptized in Jesus' name that night; then Mom and I went home.

While riding the bus back and forth to work, I prayed every day for God to fill me with the Holy Ghost. However, I wanted to receive the Holy Ghost without any shouting, dancing, or emotional outburst. I prayed for the Holy Ghost for about one month.

One Sunday night, while sitting in service during testimonies, I was crying as I stood to testify. With my eyes shut, suddenly I felt myself moving out into the aisle and walking toward the front of the church. I stopped right in front of the pulpit, facing the congregation. Everyone was quiet, so quiet—like a Catholic church. Suddenly I heard a man's voice saying, "Where is that girl's mother? It's a shame to let a young woman stand there and lose her mind."

The pastor stopped him and said, "Sit down, brother. You're out of order!" The next thing I knew, a lady came up and took me by the arm. I was lost in the Spirit. She led me to the prayer room. In the prayer room, the lady turned me over to the Lord, and I prayed through to the Holy Ghost and fire. I prayed from 9 P.M. to 1 A.M., rejoicing in God's Spirit, lying flat on my back worshiping. At 1 A.M. I spoke in other tongues as God's Spirit gave utterance, while my mother and four others prayed with me. While speaking in tongues, God called me to Honolulu, Hawaii.

At this point, I was about eighteen years old, single, living with my mother. The morning after I received the Holy Ghost, I got out of bed and looked in the mirror. Before I was saved, I would rather dance than eat. Looking in the mirror, I said, "I have no desire to dance. I have no desire to go to the theater."

I had been changed, newborn; my whole life had been rearranged. God's Spirit, not a preacher, showed me that I must not wear makeup any more. I must stop cutting my hair. I must turn from all worldly pleasures. I knew that salvation was a direct miracle from God.

The next day my mother sent me to the grocery store to make change for her. We had just moved, and I had never been in this store before. At the store, the young man behind the counter was tall and handsome. This young man's name was Oscar Vouga.

I said to him, "Tomorrow is a holiday, July 4th. I presume you are taking your wife out to dinner."

He said, "Sis, I don't have a wife. What about you going out with me?"

"Well, I guess that will be okay as I don't have anything planned."

"What show do you want to go to?"

"I don't go to shows. Let's go to the tent meeting and hear Gypsy Smith."

"That's okay," he answered.

So we went to the meeting. After service he took me home, and my mother fixed us a snack. As Oscar was saying goodnight, he made another date for Sunday dinner with his aunt, where he lived. So I went with him to dinner. That evening he brought me back to the apartment and came in to visit.

While visiting he asked, "May I put a ring on your finger?"

I answered, "Yes" as I cried with embarrassment. Oscar had already decided our wedding date. He told me he had to go to St. Louis on a business trip and was scheduled to be gone one month. We wanted to get married on August 11 after he returned.

While Oscar was gone to St. Louis, I spent much time in prayer. I prayed, "Lord, if Oscar is not the man for me, please move him out of my life completely." Oscar arrived back on Sunday, August 10. At noon on August 11, we were married.

My stepfather, who was a minister of the gospel, married Oscar and me. He told me that God had revealed to him that He was going to use Oscar Vouga in a great way.

At this point, Oscar Vouga was unsaved. Oscar had been raised as a strict Presbyterian. Oscar's whole family was very upset over Oscar's marrying a Pentecostal lady. However, Jesus had a plan for the lives of Mr. and Mrs. Oscar Vouga.

After the wedding, Oscar and I went to Santa Cruz, California, for a one-week honeymoon. We returned from our honeymoon and rented an apartment in Oakland, California, close to Oscar's work.

We attended 9th Street Mission, my home church. Since he had such a strict Presbyterian background, it took Oscar one month to see the truth. I prayed and gave him verses of Scripture to read every night when he came home from work. I would say, "Honey, please read these scriptures." As he read the Word, I could see God opening his understanding.

One Saturday night I was unable to go with Oscar to church. He went alone, but that night something got hold of Oscar Vouga. He saw the light on Jesus Name baptism. He saw that just being a good, clean-living person was not enough to save him, so Oscar was baptized in Jesus' name. The saints of the church told him that he spoke in tongues, but Oscar did not feel satisfied.

The next night after we had gone to bed, the Spirit of the Lord came upon Oscar, and he spoke in tongues for a half hour, shaking the whole bed. Then he fell asleep.

In a prayer meeting in our home a few days later, some missionaries from China came over to visit us. Brother Vouga began praying and speaking in tongues. When we arose from prayer, the missionary said, "Brother Vouga, it's so nice to hear you speak in our own Canton language." This convinced Brother Vouga that he had the Holy Ghost. From then on, he never doubted.

A few weeks later we went to Honolulu, Hawaii, as missionaries. We lived there for seven years. Brother Vouga worked for Kraft Cheese Company and preached at churches and missions and held street meetings. We helped in the churches with other missionaries.

One night in church at the altar, Brother Vouga went to pray with a Chinese woman. The next day an American lady called us and said that the Chinese woman with whom Brother Vouga had prayed asked her, "Who is the young American man that speaks such good Chinese?"

The American woman told her, "That man does not know one word of Chinese."

"But he told me how to worship God in my own language. He said I should lift my hands and praise the Lord," the woman insisted. This was the start of Brother and Sister Vouga's missionary work.

God worked many mighty miracles in Hawaii. In a humble mission one night, a young man and his family came to church. This man was blind and had never seen his baby. At the close of the service, he went to the altar for Brother Vouga to pray for his salvation. While Brother Vouga was praying, the man shouted, "I can see, I can see! I can see my baby for the first time! I've never seen my baby before! I'm going home to see the rest of my family!" For this miracle all I can say is, "To God be the glory!"

When I was twenty-one years old, while still in Hawaii, I conceived for the first time, but it was a tubal conception that burst. I hemorrhaged severely, so I was rushed to the hospital and was operated on at one o'clock in the morning. The doctor told Brother Vouga, "If your wife is here in the morning, a higher power than mine will keep her."

The next morning the doctor came into my room. I said, "I want to get up."

"No way," he answered. "Gabriel was down here last night tooting his horn for you!" From that morning I miraculously recovered and went home nine days later.

When Brother Vouga and I left Hawaii, we came back to the United States to evangelize. We started in Idaho, covering every city and church. We pastored in Nampa, Idaho. Later we pastored in Houston, Texas. Then we went to Winnipeg, Canada, and pastored and evangelized for ten years.

While in Canada many souls were saved. Some of our saints were healed of tuberculosis. Brother and Sister William Cooling were saved under Brother Vouga's ministry. When Brother Cooling went to the altar, he was an alcoholic. In one night he repented, prayed through, and was baptized in Jesus' name and received the Holy Ghost. Later Brother Vouga performed the marriage ceremony for Brother and Sister Cooling.

As for Brother Cooling's experience with God, this one night's experience he received when he prayed through has lasted all these years. Brother and Sister Cooling sat under Brother Vouga's ministry for nine years; then they went on in the Lord's work, never once looking back.

At the General Conference in 1985, I heard Brother and Sister Cooling tell Brother Sam Latta that if they had not sat under Brother Vouga's ministry all those years, they didn't know where they would be today.

Ruth Daniels Vouga

While in Winnipeg, a young lady named Dorothy Anderson had something seriously wrong with her spine and back. Mrs. Anderson had been told by doctors that she would never have children. In one of our services, Brother Vouga prayed and God performed a miracle. Her back was completely healed. Afterward Mrs. Anderson had four children.

While in Winnipeg, Brother Vouga and I adopted our only son, David Oscar Vouga. He was two and a half years old.

We left Canada and moved to Prichard, Alabama, to pastor a church. Little David said, "Mommy, this is an antichrist church." Ants were crawling all over the songbooks, not to mention the roaches playing hide and seek. The saints in Prichard were great people to work with, but they desperately needed a new church.

Brother Vouga helped them get started on a building program. We were there ten years, and before we left, we dedicated a new church building to the glory of God.

While we were there, Brother and Sister Adcock had a baby born with a club foot. The baby's foot was put in a brace, and the doctor told the Adcocks that the boy would never be able to walk except with a cane. The next Sunday, Sister Adcock fasted all day. That night I sat next to her in service. She said, "If Brother Vouga says anything tonight about healing in his message, I will take my boy up for prayer."

While preaching, Brother Vouga switched his message to the healing of the man at the Gate Beautiful. Immediately Sister Adcock took her son's brace off and walked to the front with the baby. As she stood in front of the pulpit, Brother Vouga did not ask any questions. He just got the bottle of olive oil and anointed the baby at once. While Brother Vouga was praying, the little club foot straightened out perfectly, right before the congregation. So great was the miracle that when the baby got old enough to walk, Sister Adcock told her son the story of his healing. The boy, James, looked at his feet and said, "Mom, which foot was crippled? They both look the same to me."

When James was five years old, our son, David, was backslid. One evening we were all sitting in the church fellowship hall and James was running in front of us. Brother Vouga said to his son, "David, look at this miracle." Tears ran down David's face as he remembered the night that James Adcock's club foot was healed.

While building the Prichard church and hammering on the ceiling, Brother Vouga had a mouth full of nails. While hammering, Brother Vouga spit out blue stone (deadly poison) which had been on the nails in his mouth. A man working with him said, "Brother Vouga, that's blue stone. You'll die!"

Brother Vouga answered, "No, the Bible says if I take up any deadly thing, it shall not hurt me." He kept on hammering.

A week after the church dedication, Brother Vouga was asked to go to St. Louis for a board meeting, where he was elected as the international missionary director. So we moved to St. Louis.

We toured the world together as international missionary director and wife. The way people live on the other side of the world is unforgettable, indescribable, and inexplicable. The poverty in some places is appalling.

One night after a service in Yugoslavia, one of the

English-speaking men took us to the apartment of one of the saints, where we were to spend the night. It was very cold. Before we went to bed, the lady of the house brought a pan of warm water and sat it on the floor in front of me. She couldn't speak English, so she just made signs to me. She took off my shoes and stockings and proceeded to wash my feet in the warm water before I went to bed. Her husband washed Brother Vouga's feet in warm water the same way. They would not let us remove our shoes and stockings. They wanted to do it all. It was their way of showing gratitude and hospitality. They apologized for their poverty, gave us their bed, and sat up all night themselves. In this town, there was no space in the motels, but their humble hospitality warmed our hearts. By this time it was midnight, and we had to leave at four o'clock that morning. Before we left, the American man brought us cheese and crackers for our breakfast.

While in Belgrade, Yugoslavia, when Brother Vouga got up to preach, the English interpreter said, "Brother Vouga, preach doctrine and preach long." For the entire service, six hundred people sat on backless benches, but no one moved until the preacher said, "Rise for the benediction." Then they began to leave. A Russian spy attended every service.

While in foreign countries, Brother Vouga and I heard many people, who knew no English, speak in plain English as they received the Holy Ghost.

Once we were in a service in Thailand with Brother Cole when he said, "See that lady you hear speaking in English right now? She can't even say, 'Hello,' in English." What a beautiful experience!

Brother Vouga served as international missionary

director for seven years. As a pioneer and one of the founders of United Pentecostal Church, he had also filled the office of general secretary and assistant general superintendent under Brother Howard A. Goss. During this time we saw many souls saved and healed.

When Brother Vouga finished his position as international missionary director, he received a call to pastor a church in Macon, Georgia. We pastored in Macon for seven years until Brother Vouga's death.

During his sickness, God blessed us with a wonderful church family. The saints saw to it that we were well cared for.

When we had to move, the saints moved us into our new home. Before we arrived, the saints had everything in place: furniture, pictures, dishes. All we had to do was walk in and go to bed as though we had always lived there. As we walked in for the first time, the saints greeted us at the door singing, "Welcome home!" We lived in the new home for three years.

Brother Vouga became ill and was hospitalized. While in the hospital, he died four times. Doctors were amazed at the miracles God did in his life. One of the doctors said, "If you hear that he's bleeding to death, don't believe it!"

Brother Vouga's last desire was to visit the foreign missionary field one more time before his death. Brother and Sister Thompson invited Brother Vouga to South America to preach a conference. Brother C. L. Dees of Houston, Texas, went with us to look after Brother Vouga.

The fact that Brother Vouga survived this trip is a miracle. Many people were filled with the Holy Ghost during the meeting. Jesus kept His hand on us and brought us back to the United States safely. After returning, Brother

Vouga died August 8, 1976, at age 75.

After Brother Vouga's death, I moved to Houston, Texas, into a home across the street from Brother Dees's church. I lived there five years. Those were hard, lonely days, but God gave me many friends. One young lady, Cindy Castlebury, grew so close that I claimed her as my adopted daughter.

One day I was at the Houston airport coffee shop, pushing a tray with my breakfast on it. A gentleman behind me asked, "Are you going to have a drink with your egg?"

I said, "Yes, I am going to have coffee."

"Can I get it for you?" he asked.

"Yes, of course," I replied.

He was gone for quite some time. When he returned, he explained, "I was looking for a clean cup." After he got my coffee, I went into the dining room, but the man had disappeared.

I left Houston and moved to Valdosta, Georgia, for one year. My next move was to Atlanta, Georgia, to settle in a home situation with security. Brother and Sister James McGee remodeled their home, making me a three-room apartment attached to their house. Brother and Sister McGee have been a real blessing in my life. I am on my own, although I am not alone as my apartment is attached to their home through the kitchen door.

Although I have been a widow since Brother Vouga's death, God has shown His love and care for me in many ways.

At the General Conference right after my husband's death, God began to perform miracles in my life to let me know that He was with me. When I arrived at Salt Lake

City for the conference, I met a couple at the airport. They were very friendly to me and said, "We are going to take you in our car to the hotel where you are staying." This couple stayed at the registration desk until I was completely checked in. Then the man took a card out of his wallet and said, "If you need us at anytime, call me, and we will be at your service."

One morning while preparing to go to the convention hall, I had to get a taxi alone. No one but Jesus was with me. A young Australian man got into the front seat of the same taxi as I got into the back seat. I said to the taxi driver, "Let me know how much I owe when you get to the convention hall." The young man in the front seat, a total stranger to me, said, "Driver, take her where she wants to go, then take me where I'm going, and I will pay the whole bill." I breathed, "Thank you, Jesus. This is my first miracle!"

At the same conference on Sunday afternoon, someone tapped me on the shoulder and said, "Come with me to the Harvestime banquet."

I replied, "I have money to pay, but I don't have a ticket."

When we arrived at the banquet, they didn't want to let me in even if I offered to pay. However, some young man saw me standing there, rushed over, and said, "Sister Vouga, come with me." He took me to one of the front tables and sat me with Brother and Sister Chambers and Brother and Sister Kinzie. The banquet didn't cost me anything; that was another miracle that showed me that wherever I go and whatever I do, Jesus will be with me.

Yes, as the song says, "His eye is on the sparrow, and I know He watches me." You see, after losing my lifetime companion, I felt as though no one cared. But Jesus used people, some total strangers, to show me that He cared and was watching over me. Jesus understood my loneliness.

*　*　*　*　*

Judy Williams, the writer of Sister Vouga's story, tells some of her memories of this unique lady.

As a twelve-year-old child, I grew up in Brother Guy Roam's church in University City, Missouri. During this time Brother Vouga was foreign missionary director. Brother and Sister Vouga would visit Brother Roam's church quite frequently. Brother Vouga would preach, and Sister Vouga would sing and testify.

I remember Sister Vouga saying in one testimony, "Honey, if I had a skirt on that I had to fight with, I'd leave it hanging in the closet." (That must have been in the days of mini-skirts.) She also urged us to pray more, saying, "We have Chinese, Japanese, and American knees." Truly she was a unique, unforgettable lady.

Here is one of her favorite songs:

Three Thousand Million Souls Are Dying

Three thousand million souls are dying,
Three thousand million souls for whom my Savior
　died.
Can you still deny their pleas?
Can you longer idle be,
While three thousand million souls are dying?

This is another song she enjoyed singing.

A Humorous Scottish Chorus

Cheer up, ye saints of God!
There's nothing to worry about.
There's nothing to make you feel afraid,
Nothing to make you doubt.
Remember God is on the throne;
Why not trust Him and shout?
You'll be sorry you worried at all tomorrow morning.

by Judy Williams

*The store in Oakland, California,
where Sister Vouga invited Brother Vouga
to the tent meeting.*

Brother and Sister Vouga in Honolulu, Hawaii, in May 1932

Brother and Sister Vouga in Nampa, Idaho in 1932

Brother and Sister Vouga at their 50th wedding anniversary on August 11, 1974